one dad

encountering God

Text copyright © Brad Lincoln 2010
The author asserts the moral right
to be identified as the author of this work

Published by
The Bible Reading Fellowship
15 The Chambers, Vineyard
Abingdon OX14 3FE
United Kingdom
Tel: +44 (0)1865 319700
Email: enquiries@brf.org.uk
Website: www.brf.org.uk
BRF is a Registered Charity

ISBN 978 1 84101 678 8

First published 2010
10 9 8 7 6 5 4 3 2 1 0
All rights reserved

Acknowledgments
Unless otherwise stated, scripture quotations are taken from the Holy Bible, New International
Version, copyright © 1973, 1978, 1984 by International Bible Society, and are used by
permission of Hodder & Stoughton Publishers, a member of the Hachette Livre UK Group.
All rights reserved. 'NIV' is a registered trademark of International Bible Society. UK trademark
number 1448790.

A catalogue record for this book is available from the British Library

Printed in Singapore by Craft Print International Ltd

one dad

encountering God

Brad Lincoln

For Joshua, Zoë and Jed, who teach me so much—
not least that simple pleasures outweigh complex problems.
Thank you.

❖

Preface

Why?

God speaks to us every day but we don't know how to listen.
Mahatma Gandhi

I live 'a life of quiet desperation'. I am weaker than I want ever to admit. I want so much to be peaceful, to be fulfilled, to be whole. My day-to-day life, however, brings manifold reminders of my failure to live up to my own mediocre standards—far short of Jesus' benchmark.

I want, unrealistically, to be a perfect friend and husband and disciple and son. I am not. I am an unremarkable man. I am a father.

Even so, I've had the great pleasure and privilege to do some unusual things, and I believe that some of my experiences have encouraged me to take a new perspective on the world I meet. Living as a missionary in Nepal for a number of years helped me to develop a better understanding of what it is to have and what it is to be without, and the TV-less evenings gave me time to reflect on the challenges with which real poverty assaulted me. In the same way, having three children of my own forced me to consider and appreciate more the parenting I myself had received. In some cases these experiences were combined, such as learning to speak Nepali while watching my first child grasping at his first words, and often the struggles in one would amplify the wonder of the other.

I would sometimes find it easier to understand these

moments by jotting them down. I write—not just this book—for that reason. My motives are not selfless. I write not to leave a legacy or to make my parents proud; not to communicate any truths or wisdom I may have gained or to give anyone the benefit of what little I know or understand. I write because writing expresses me. In spilling out my thoughts, I hope somehow to learn, to process what is inside, to earn some inner calm. Many times I may blame my children for robbing me of moments of reflection with their interruptions, but I find that when the quietness does come, it is the moments with them that I reflect on most.

I write, also, because for some reason that is how I pray. I write down even my daily prayers, expecting no one ever to read them. I write because it allows me to hurl myself on to a blank page and make myself vulnerable. I write in the hope that at least God will understand.

If I truly am unremarkable, then I must assume that many others, some who would rather read than write, also feel a certain dissatisfaction. I offer this book to all who want so much in this life, who are greedy for answers and know deep within that there is more. I hope you, like me, believe that, with all other avenues explored, it can only be God who holds out the promise of a life worth living. In this life I am temporarily comforted, I have brief insights, I have flashes of joy and precious moments of love. I choose to believe that these are glimpses of the divine and that life with God offers to fit these jigsaw pieces together, to make me perfect and whole.

I have come to the conclusion that only God can lift me out of the ordinary. I am impatient for his answers.

Contents

Introduction

What if?

My Me is God, nor do I recognise any other Me except my God Himself.

Saint Catherine of Genoa

How would my life be different if I really understood God?

What if, instead of a muddle of ideas and half-thought-through concepts jumbled together, a mess of Sunday school images and media caricatures, I carried around inside my head a real concrete image of God that I could relate to?

OK, maybe God is far too complex and beautiful and powerful for me to really get a mental image of him. So what if, in the same way that Jesus used simple metaphors to explain concepts of the kingdom of heaven, I had a simple metaphor that at least communicated the key points to me?

Oh, sure, I'd have to accept that the simple metaphor would not be a comprehensive picture of God and the way he relates to me, but if it just pointed me in the right direction, wouldn't that help?

If there was such a metaphor, it would have to be something I understood fully, something I grasped intimately. It would also have to be an image I could carry with me at all times, familiar but also able to show me a new facet of God whenever I took a moment to look past its familiarity to see what it might be telling me about him. What if God gave me something like that to help me decipher him?

If he did, it would need to be a picture that involved

relationship with another being, so that I could use it to understand a little better how he relates to people. No, wait—what if I could use it to understand what he might be saying to me?

So I'm looking for a metaphor in which one element is (perhaps imperfectly) displaying qualities of God, such as power and knowledge and control and discipline, to another element that is somehow less in all of those areas. I know that God is love,[1] so the 'bigger' element has to show love for the lesser element of the metaphor, and that love must be the closest thing to perfect love that I can comprehend, mustn't it?

Now that I think about it, it occurs to me that so much of life is about emotions, so God would have to give me a picture that I could really feel as well as know first-hand. Then I'd want to talk to others about the metaphor, to discuss it, to chew it over, so that I could get others' views and insights on the concepts it showed me. So it would have to be an image that everyone, or almost everyone, could relate to, like the sun or water—something universal.

If only God had given us a metaphor like that. Wouldn't it be great?

But what if he already has? What if it's here somewhere, if only I could find it?

What if it was so close to me that I could touch it? In fact, what if it was so close to me that it was inside me?

It would have to be something so simple and so universal—like being a father, or being a child.

Given that God is everywhere and in everything, perhaps birds and bees, mountains and marmosets, clouds and ocean

---

[1] 1 John 4:16

currents might provide sufficient material to reflect upon. If I had enough direct experience, maybe I could have developed a deeper understanding of God by considering them? But it just so happens that I have spent more time in the last eight-and-a-half years being a father than anything else, and even though that is nowhere near enough to make me a fathering expert, perhaps it has at least given me the rich source of experiences I need to tap into. What I do know is that being a father is a gift from God[2] and could be the closest I will ever get to understanding how he feels about me.

From the very first seconds of fatherhood—the sublime mixture of relief at the safe delivery of a healthy baby and an overwhelming sense of new responsibility—I've been made aware of a new world. If God feels that way about me, then I suspect he has been taking a closer interest in me than I normally give him credit for.

What if, in my own fatherhood, he has given me the perfect explanation of himself?

I pray that through these reflections you get a sense of him and his fatherhood.

---

[2] Psalm 127:3

❖

Chapter One

Knowing God

Knowing

Real knowledge is to know the extent of one's ignorance.

Confucius

I don't think I know God that well at all. I've met him—not as often as I would like, but we've had our encounters; we have a relationship. It's not as close as it should be. We spend time together—which is to say that I spend a lot of time looking for him—but sometimes I'm not sure if I meet him. Occasionally, very occasionally, I hear him with crystal clarity, but again, not as often as I'd like. More frequently, when I think I've heard his voice I have a vague suspicion that it might be an echo of my own—or, worse, the voice of someone deliberately misleading me. You'd think, after all this time, I would know what he sounded like but, no, I don't think I could say that I actually *know* God very well at all.

There have been times in my Christian journey, mostly early on, when I said that I knew him, but I always felt slightly uncomfortable when I did so. It felt as though I was using the word 'know' in a different way, almost as if it was another piece of jargon in the Christian lexicon that we all have to learn when we start attending church, going to house groups and reading daily Bible study notes. I *know* my wife, my children, my sister, my parents, and I know precisely what I mean when I say that. In most situations I know pretty much what my wife is thinking, and I love that. I can look at her back—perhaps as she is washing dishes at the sink—and, by the way she is standing, the way she holds her shoulders or by the way she brushes some hair back from her face, I know how she is feeling. I probably watch her, study her, more often than she realises, and I love the feeling I get from knowing that I know her.

There are three people in the world whom I've observed so intimately that I can pick them out in a crowd silhouetted on the horizon just by the way they stand or move one of their limbs. I know their favourite colours, foods, games, TV programmes and pyjamas. I know how to make them laugh, what frightens them, their friends and their horrible habits. I could say without fear of contradiction that I am one of the world's top two experts on my children.

I know my mother well, too. I know the special code she uses when she telephones to ask, some time in early August, what our plans are for Christmas, and I know that she has her own ideas. I know she won't tell me exactly what they are for fear of imposing, and I know that if I phone my sister, she will be able to tell me what Mum is thinking. I know that Dad always laughs at Tom and Jerry cartoons, and that if he picks up the phone he will want to tell me about the last round of golf he played. I've spent a lifetime relating to these people, living with them, making mistakes and learning about them. When they call me on the phone I don't have to ask or guess who it is because I already know. I know them.

I hope (I don't absolutely know) that God has got a sense of humour, because I am about to compare him to Richard Branson. You see, sometimes it feels to me as if, in my relationship with God, I am like a relatively low-level employee in Virgin Atlantic or on Virgin Trains. Imagining myself as that employee, I've read about Sir Richard; I might even have met him. I've heard others talk about him; I've spoken to people who have spent more time with him. I could be said to serve him: I live a certain part of my life within a system of which he sits at the head, a system that has certain rules of behaviour, and I even depend on him (or, at least, the managers to whom he delegates) for my daily bread in the form of a monthly salary. His communications team pass me messages from him, his decisions affect me, and somewhere in his Human Resources department is a file that records all the significant events in my career. I might even be one of those lucky employees invited to the annual party at the Branson house and, while there, get to shake his hand or chat with him briefly. Even so, I don't think many of the Virgin team could honestly say that they know Sir Richard Branson.

The act of admitting that I am perhaps only an acquaintance of God feels like a big step, mainly because I seem to meet many, many Christians who tell me that they do know God. I have a suspicion that these people fall into three categories.

I think the largest category is of those who substitute 'know' for 'believe in'. When they ask if you 'know Jesus', they are asking if you believe in Jesus, if you have become a Christian. When they say that they 'know God', they are confessing their belief—but that's not the same as knowing. I believe Richard Branson exists and, if I were his employee, I might even be said to trust him for certain things. However, if I were to speculate about why he persists with that goatee or the quirky personal appearances when he launches a new product, it would be purely that—speculation.

I think the next largest group comprises mainly new Christians who think they know God. I've been there myself and, if I am honest, I envy them that fresh-faced, un-complicated, exhilarating belief that they have discovered

God and know him. I can remember the breathless realisation that God offers a personal relationship, holding out his hand towards me; and, having seized his hand and experienced my first close encounter with him, I met him properly for the first time. In my excitement I might even have said that I knew him, in the same way that a lucky Virgin employee leaving the Branson drinks party after a 15-second encounter might well tell a mate down the pub that he knew Richard.

I am older and (sadly) more sober now. The more I learn about God, the more I realise I have to learn. But because of that—and here is the point—I really want to know God. I want to know him, to understand him, to get more than a brief glimpse of him, to know him so well that I understand what he is thinking. I want to speak to him and discern that he has a plan. Even if he doesn't want to tell me what it is, I want to be able to gather enough clues to get an idea of what he has in mind. I want to know what he feels, loves, likes, laughs at, hates and enjoys. I want to know what he likes about me and what he gently ignores or tolerates. I want a depth of relationship far greater than that described by those who carelessly toss the word 'know' into an account of their experience of God. I want to become a member of that third category of people, who can say they truly know God.

Just pause with me a moment and think what that would be like. I'm not quite sure I can imagine it, but perhaps you can. Focus on how it would feel to hear God's footstep as he approached and know that it was his; to see an expression of recognition flicker across his face as he met your eyes. Imagine seeing in those eyes an enduring love, a perfect empathy. Imagine being completely understood. Envisage being humoured but not patronised as you make your necessary mistakes, all the while knowing that, having fallen, you will be set back on your feet and dusted down, your skinned knees kissed better. Imagine having immediate access to perfect advice on all of the most important issues you face, while knowing that the advice will never be forced upon you, but will be held available for the moment when you decide you are ready to ask. Think of knowing with total certainty that you will always be given the rest, food and companionship you need. Imagine understanding that, from time to time, you will be presented with challenges sufficient to help you grow and develop but never beyond your ability, stretching you, but never to breaking point. Imagine knowing God.

Is that what Adam and Eve experienced in the heavenly time before they ate the forbidden fruit? They certainly knew the sound of God's approach, and surely it was the cause of delight rather than fear and embarrassment, as it later became. To be honest, my attempts at picturing those early days in the garden are hampered by the images of manicured fruit trees, lawns and rose bushes. I don't for one minute believe it was anything like that, given the sort of rugged, earthy beauty God seems to prefer in the wild parts of his creation that we have yet to fully possess, but the memories of those Renaissance paintings are hard to shake off.

Of course, there is no contemporary equivalent on earth to this perfect Father–child relationship, but there are fleeting glimpses in our normal healthy experiences. I can recall, as a child, winning a minor race at a family fun day: having broken the tape, I looked up to see my dad's face amid the crowd of parents. There was a look of recognition and approval stretching across the space between us that needed no words. There are times when I ask my own children what they've done at school that day and, instead of the more common shrugged response, they take delight in my interest and in sharing with me some new discovery. These are glimpses of perfection.

Having said that, though, I prefer the somewhat more challenging image of 'knowing' conjured up by that friend of God, Abraham.[1] Imagine his level of certainty as he obeyed God's voice, strapping his only son to a hastily constructed altar and raising a knife above him, ready to sacrifice his sole heir.[2] This man—this human, real, flesh-and-blood man—had enough confidence in God's promise that he was prepared to sweep away the only reasonable route through which it could be fulfilled for no other practical reason than as a demonstration of his faith. As Abraham stood there, smelling the sweat and hearing the short gasps of his terrified son, feeling the cool weight of the sacrificial knife in his trembling hands; as he squeezed his eyes shut, clenched his jaw and tensed ready for the blow; as time and the world paused, was he unshaken in his knowledge of his loving friend, Yahweh?

Surely Abraham must have had doubts. Did he wrestle with the idea that this inner voice, telling him to do terrible, inconceivable things, was a symptom of madness seizing him? Even if he didn't question God, surely he must have questioned his own mental health. Of course he would have stood there, waiting for God to intervene. Did he know God so well that he expected a stay of execution, recognising that the act demanded of him was not in keeping with God's true personality? It may seem strange that I prefer this moment of turmoil to many of the gentler Bible stories of lost sheep found and wounds healed, but it speaks to me of real knowing. No matter what Abraham expected, no matter how hard he wrestled internally, his actions can only have been those of a man who absolutely knew his God and his God's voice.

You might be thinking that if that is what it takes to really

---

[1]   See Isaiah 41:8
[2]   Genesis 22:2–10

know God, then ignorance is bliss. I don't see myself as a budding Abraham and I don't even pretend to know exactly what was going on in the drama described in Genesis, but to hear God so clearly and with such a degree of certainty— now that would be something. To know God and to trust that, whatever happened, it would be for the best (or, unlike Jonah, to know fully that any attempt to thwart God's plans would be futile) speaks of real intimacy and understanding.

The Bible is full of the rewards of such knowledge. If I knew God this well, would I see modern-day equivalents of walls tumbling, promised lands opening up, prison doors flung open and visions of heaven so wonderful that they can be expressed only in mythical metaphor? Perhaps not, but I'd settle for a certain knowledge that, far beyond our dreary trudge through a poisoned world in which money does the only talking to which people pay attention, I could see the grand plan and the fulfilment of God's promises of peace and beauty and power and holy passion. I'd be happy with enough vision to see the spiritual impact of my prayers, to know that he rejoices when I do the right thing, and to know which way to look when I am uncertain or tempted.

I don't believe that I can fully know God, but I do so want to know him better.

Wanting to want

If you don't get what you want, it's a sign that either you did not seriously want it, or that you tried to bargain over the price.
Rudyard Kipling

Normally this is the point in the chapter at which the author presents you, the reader, with some practical advice: study your Bible more, read some commentaries, find a place and a time for quiet reflection, buy some daily notes, get into a prayer triplet, go on a retreat, do some fasting, reflect.

And so you should. These disciplines are important—vital, even—to our development in understanding God and our own faith. I have been doing these things for years; indeed, I am still doing them. I work assiduously at my prayer life, blocking out time each morning to pray about the day ahead and my relationship with God. I use the tactic, recommended by Billy Graham, of reading a psalm every day to deepen my relationship with God. I use a devotional guide (an online one, this being the 21st century) to guide me into different parts of the Bible, to discover new insights of my own or those of the authors. I have written a Life Purpose Statement and I read a sentence from it every day, as well as setting aside half a day every six weeks to review it and look for evidence of that purpose in my life and my time commitments. Speaking of that, I set aside half an hour every Friday morning to check that the following week's appointments include sufficient activities that correspond to the priorities I want to have in my life. I read commentaries and guidance written by authors such as Philip Yancey and John Eldredge and James Lawrence and Henri Nouwen. I keep a daily prayer diary, and my Bible is littered with notes and references and insights.

If there is one area where I am especially weak, it is in praying with others, but I'm even working on that. I've recently found a friend I respect and with whom I believe I can be open and vulnerable, who has agreed to work with me so that we can be mutually accountable and support each other on our spiritual journeys. (If you are reading this, thanks, Jon!)

Is all this working? Yes.

As I have invested heavily in time and effort, getting to

know God, I have grown in my understanding. I'm still very much a work in progress but I can look back with great affection on times when the effort has been rewarded. There was a period of six weeks when I found myself living alone in the Nepali border town of Nepalgunj. I would get up each day, make a cup of coffee and sit on my flat roof to watch the sun creep over the horizon. I'd start by just watching the sky brighten to a pale blue over the grubby houses, trying to concentrate on getting a sense of the presence of God.[3] My mind would wander from time to time, or I'd be distracted by my neighbour spreading runner beans or peas out on her roof to dry, by the mangy street dogs scavenging in the piles of litter or by the jostle of children kicking up the dust on the way to school. But I would try not to let these disturbances bother me and instead would look for the handiwork of the Creator in even the most mundane. Then, after a while, I'd turn to my Bible, read a few verses and run through the expected events of the coming day in my mind, parading them in front of God and asking for his blessing or his advice.

I don't believe that at any time I heard a direct literal answer or instruction but, when I climbed down the steps before heading out to work, I was able to carry a sense of the spiritual with me into my day. Too often, of course, it evaporated in the heat and hurry, on some days more quickly than on others, but I knew it would be restored, perhaps a fraction more durably, on the next morning.

Up until that time I'd failed to get a consistent quiet time routine going, even though I knew I should. I'd tried various Bible notes, various times of day and various locations, all

---

[3] I heartily recommend a book by John White called *The Fight: A Practical Handbook for Christian Living* (IVP, 2008, first published 1976) for practical advice on how to go about focusing on God.

without success for longer than perhaps a couple of weeks. Pretty quickly I'd get fed up. Until then, I knew I should be investing in knowing God better but I did not seem able to put in the effort. It wasn't so much that I wanted to know God better; it was that I wanted to want to know him.

However, after a while I began to find that if, for some reason, I did miss my daily dose of devotions, I didn't feel guilty but I did feel the loss. I had come to rely on the peace, the inner sense of calm and purpose that seemed to grow during the quiet times, and days that started without it were just not as good. I became addicted to it. I found I was embracing anything that could give me a deeper insight into God and my relationship with him.

People often say that the secret to developing a healthy relationship—whether as a husband, wife, parent, child or good friend—is to spend quality time together. However, just try calling up someone you haven't spoken to for years and inviting them over for some 'quality time'. Chances are, it won't be straightforward. Even now I can 'hear' the embarrassing silence as the small talk is exhausted and, in the absence of shared experience, there is nothing more to say. In the same way that a vibrant prayer life rarely springs into being on the first day you commit to morning devotions, and in the same way that an absent father can't immediately and easily engage with his children, so quality time comes only as a result of quantity time. The walk to school, kicking a ball in the park, even watching TV together, all work to get fathers relating to their sons and daughters.

If you are hoping to find in the following pages a quick-fix solution, a short cut to heavenly insight, then I am delighted to disappoint you. This book would be far more radical and controversial if I were to suggest that the Quiet Time is dead, that Bible study is outdated and that there is another way, but it turns out that those wiser, more mature, more learned Christians than I, who have been recommending those disciplines for years, are in fact right. Sorry.

Head and heart

I believe in God. If you were me, and had my life, you would believe in God too.

Michael Caine, *Sunday Times*, 23 December 2001

My problem is that I am what they call an activist: I learn best not by thinking about things but by experiencing them. This infuriates my wife frequently. If she tells me that a plate is hot, I still have to touch it to check for myself. Contrary to the way it must seem, it's not that I don't believe her; it's just that I seem to need to feel the heat and sometimes get burnt for myself before I fully grasp the truth. I can read the Bible from cover to cover (indeed, I have done) and I can find written there the characteristics of God. I can read that he is slow to anger, abounding in love, powerful, forgiving, worthy of praise, and that he delights in me, and I am encouraged. While I can hold that information in my mind, at the front of my consciousness, it affects how I feel and how I behave, but as soon as I return to autopilot my unconscious worldview takes over.

I have read a thousand times that God will provide for me, that I am more valuable than so many sparrows and lilies, but when I look at my diminishing bank account and insecure income I worry about paying the mortgage. On my good days, I can see the red numbers on the bank statement, hand them over to God and go about my work with nothing more than a mildly nagging sense of concern. On my bad days, the problem looms large, casting a shadow over everything else, destroying my concentration, feeding my irritation and robbing me of peace. Oh, me of little faith! The promises haven't changed but I don't think I have really taken them right down into my heart. They just tend to float around in my head.

It occurred to me that God would know this, having designed me. If I am wired this way, and if God really does want me to grow in more than a purely theoretical understanding of him, then he will have to give me practical examples of how this relationship works—examples that I can experience and feel and respond to. I need experiences in which I can get burnt, in which I can taste small triumphs and struggle with failures. If I am to learn more about how God deals with me and gain insights into the way his mind and heart work, I am probably going to need some practical examples to go with all the theoretical data I am stuffing into my head. And, if God really does know me, surely he is going to provide the opportunities, if I can just find them.

Just pause and look back at the paragraph that starts 'Focus on how it would feel' on page 14. Read again what it would be like to know God that well. As I use my imagination, it begins to sound more and more like having a relationship with a perfect father. That, of itself, is perhaps not an especially startling insight. Hold the front page: God is like a heavenly father! I do get another response, though. As I think through the words, I begin to realise that, as well as describing God, I am describing the impossibly perfect father I would so love to be to my own children. With that thought comes a flash of insight, along with a jumbled rush of understanding that God and I have something in common: we both want to be perfect fathers. Though unattainable, the *desire* to be a perfect father is something I can relate to.

I want to be the father who is always there, who always provides, who supports his children through their mistakes, helping them to grow. I know, innately, that to be that sort of father I need to discipline and teach them, sometimes leave them to make their own discoveries, and frequently deny them things that they want. I want my children to develop and I know that they should behave with respect.

My fallen humanity prevents me from being perfect, of course, but my desire to be a perfect father does provide me with a framework within which to relate to God. On a daily basis, God is perfectly doing all those fatherly things: choosing not to answer my inappropriate prayers, recognising my genuine achievements with appropriate rewards, listening to my questions but trying to let me work out my own answers, or giving answers when required. It also occurs to me that I often understand about as much of all this as my two-year-old son does when his mother correctly refuses to let him use the kitchen scissors. Neither he nor I is above responding with an irrational tantrum.

As I think about this further, I begin to see better in myself the imperfect child.

Little mirrors

A humble knowledge of thyself is a surer way to God than the deepest search after science.
Thomas à Kempis

'Mister Stupid.' That was my two-year-old son calling me names again, and to be honest I didn't know how best to respond. Of course, the language was inappropriate, but the attitude wasn't. Jed has been going through a phase of giving everyone the epithet 'Mister' and, because Jed is our third, I've grown used to the concept of passing phases—where, for a day or a week or even a month, a particular word becomes fashionable. These little stages are normally charming mileposts, and I've lost count of them. Many of them are endearing. Some stick in the mind, like Joshua calling his uncle Michael 'Uncle Mo-mo'. I remember it partly because Mike is pretty short, and it seemed somehow appropriate.

There is nothing especially remarkable, then, about going through the day hearing Jed speak to Mister Daddy, Mister Mummy, Mister Doogie (the dog), Mister Sid (teddy), Mister Zoë (his sister), Mister Trampoline and, inexplicably, Mister Smiksty (before you ask, I haven't a clue). And so it goes on: you get the idea.

'Stupid', though—now that is another matter. That word is a taboo in our household, a prohibited word. At least, it's prohibited except when I use it. That sounds like a double standard, doesn't it? Well, it isn't, because I am allowed to call myself stupid (for forgetting my car keys), and I am permitted to call a badly designed product 'stupid' (when I turn on my TV, a small green LED comes on, presumably because the fact that it is showing me a TV programme is not enough evidence). I am especially allowed to call companies 'stupid' (because they don't understand that I prefer speaking to real people: if they did, they would give me the option to 'press 5 if you never again want to listen to a list of options none of which quite fits your particular circumstances'). Those are the only circumstances in which the word is permitted.

So I should be angry that Jed has called me stupid. Or should I? I know he doesn't actually think I am stupid. This is the same little boy who is sometimes so excited when I come home that he jumps up and down on the spot and laughs because he doesn't have the words to explain his delight (although on other occasions he completely ignores me because Iggle Piggle is on the TV, and Iggle Piggle outranks me by some distance). He also knows that I am the person to come to for really important stuff, like fixing plastic toys, finding new batteries, putting on shoes and unwrapping sweets.

More significant than that, though, is his tone. He thinks he is being funny. There's nothing aggressive or resentful about his manner, and his smile is a cheeky grin pasted on a face of expectation. It's not a face ready to flinch because he knows he has done something deserving of punishment or reproof, and he's not challenging me. He's wanting me to play, to join in, to laugh with him.

Within me, however, I feel the rising response. The word he has used is disrespectful and he must be taught to respect me. His words are rude and he must be taught to be polite. He has insulted me. Actually, the way I feel, it is not so much that he has insulted me personally but more that he has insulted my parenting. Surely, if I was raising him correctly, if I was teaching and disciplining him in the right way, he should be standing before me as a perfect shining example of good manners. He has, in fact, touched the place deep within me that lies unmentioned, that small itchy spot that irritates me, my lingering fear that I am not doing this parenting thing right, that in the area of most importance I am failing.

How do you respond to being called a failure? Are you one of those Olympic-standard athletes in the personality game, who just humbly knuckles down and tries harder? I'm afraid I am more of the wounded tiger type, who instinctively wants to lash out, to deny the charge—except when I am tired, that is, when I just want to shove the issue under the carpet and deal with it another day. So I am embarrassed to admit that sometimes when Jed calls me names, I scold him—initially not with a raised voice, but if my response does not elicit a visible display of remorse I am prepared to turn up the volume.

How did my child learn to call people names? Actually, he got it from me. I call people names all the time, especially in my family. I don't suppose an hour goes by without me calling one of the children 'muscles' or 'sausage' or 'pickle' or 'monster' or 'chunky monkey' or 'superstar' or 'princess' or 'sunshine' or something. I don't call people 'stupid', of course, at least not within earshot of my children. The point is that I (mostly) use names appropriately as terms of endearment, and Jed has worked out that this name-calling business is OK. He doesn't think I am actually stupid any more than I think he is really a sausage, and he has got some learning to do. In the meantime, it seems he is just reflecting a slightly distorted version of my own behaviour back at me. He is an imperfect reflection.

If I am on the ball enough to work all this out in the seconds when the interaction takes place, I am able to suppress my barked response and instead see his behaviour for what it is. I can respond to his delight in seeing me and his affection, and then take the time to explain why 'we don't call people "stupid"'.

I'd like to tell you that I handled the moment this wonderfully when it actually happened. I didn't. Some time later, however, when my wife had pointed out the insights that I am writing down here as my own, I began to think about that idea of the imperfect reflection. If my son throws back an imperfect reflection of me as I muddle through as a 'good enough' father (I hope), might I be throwing back an imperfect reflection of God? If I were able to stand back and look at how I behave as a father—or rather, how I feel I should behave—might that not give me a better understanding of what God is playing at in the way he relates to me? As a byproduct, a careful examination of my own children might give me some additional and perhaps lightly chastening insights into how well I handle his fathering. Just as my wife is keen to read parenting books and pass on the received wisdom, I have to be careful to check my imperfect experiences against 'The Manual', but it might be interesting.

I hope you'll join me, and I promise not to call you 'stupid'!

Chapter Two

Love

Good and bad dads

Whoever has not a good father should procure one.
Friedrich Nietzsche

It is easy to become a father, but very difficult to be a father.
Wilhelm Busch

I'm one of the lucky ones. When I hear God described as a father, it doesn't rake up a silt of negative emotions or terrifying memories, clouding my life. I am aware that some people have experiences of abusive, absent or ambivalent fathers, and the idea that God could be anything like them is too abhorrent to consider. I can't even imagine what it must be like to live with a reality so broken and distorted, so different from the nurturing, supportive relationship that a child has the right to expect from a father. What I do know is that the consequences of this betrayal last long and perhaps never fully heal.

Partly for that reason, I am asking you not to think about your experience of being fathered; instead I want you to focus more on the type of parent you know you should be. This, too, may be challenging and difficult. For some people who have been badly treated by parents, the cycle of destructive behaviour is not just irreversible but also seemingly unstoppable, and they find themselves repeating the behaviours they themselves found so damaging. Actually, all of us who reflect even casually on our parenting style will find elements that we are not happy about, and some of us will worry about the effect we are having on our sons and daughters, fearing that we are perpetuating (or, worse, initiating) some character flaw destined to spread down through the generations like a persistent genetic trait. You may feel that the traits you pass on are somehow worse than those you perceive in others, but remember that your understanding of such things is bound to be defective.

In my family, there are some who clearly have a predisposition to self-destructive behaviour. Within each of the three generations of which I have direct experience, it manifests itself in different ways, from self-doubt, through depression, to the misuse of certain substances. Some members of the family have succumbed to the force that seems to suck at their lives, while others have battled it with varying degrees of success. Some of them envy those who seem, to the outside world, to escape such burdens and have few struggles. One such branch of my family is outwardly successful and happy but lives with a powerful sense of never being quite good enough. This can be evident in a driven nature or a striving for perfection, but always with dissatisfaction—a belief that whatever has been attained, there must always be something better and more.

We observe these traits, and we may express a preference: 'Better be someone who is driven than someone who, as a result of experiencing extreme highs and lows, turns to drink as a means of escape.' But God does not perceive us in that way. Not only does he perfectly perceive what is going on inside us[1] but he also understands the elements that went

---

[1]   1 Samuel 16:7

into making us.[2] He also seems to judge us not by what we are but by what we do with the raw material we have been given. In fact, if Jesus is anything to go by, he actually seemed to prefer those who wrestled with demons and deficiencies. As a 'friend of sinners', a man who ate and drank enough to earn the accusation of being a glutton and a drunkard,[3] Jesus freely associated with those who must have been weak in some aspect of their lives. On the other hand, Jesus also chose those who were driven souls, fierce and competitive. Surely Peter was a competitive man, not satisfied with being just one of the Twelve but striving to be *the* disciple, promising a level of performance that he could not hope to achieve. It seems unlikely to me that this was pure selflessness on his part, but rather a normal response of the male ego.

My point is that God does not seem to choose his friends and favoured children on the basis of a league table of sins. I presume that no one could seriously regard themselves as being wholly good or perfect, and that everyone would acknowledge a certain degree of fallibility. So no one should imagine themselves to be such a 'bad' father that there is nothing of God in them. Nor can we believe that any of us is inherently better than anyone else. We may make bad choices; we may receive the talents that God grants us and the many opportunities that life gives us, and squander the lot.

However, if I take the working thesis that God is the perfect father, then my deficiencies are just as instructive as the things I get right. This is not a book about how to be a better dad, but it is suggesting that, regardless of whether

---

2   Psalm 139:13
3   Luke 7:34

I am a good or bad dad, by reflecting on my own qualities I might be able to understand better what God is doing. In fact, I might start to recognise why, in so many crucial ways, he is different from my own father and different from me; in particular, I might grow to understand that, given his complete absence of neurosis, the neuroses that I have did not come from him.

I must acknowledge, though, that there are some qualities in me that I would quite like to pass on to my children: I'm not all bad! Just as there are many qualities in my wife that I delight to see being replicated in our offspring, I'm sometimes quite pleased to hear that, in some respect or another, my children are described as being a chip off this particular old block. So perhaps we should consider which of his characteristics God notices developing in us, and think about how he may glow with pride as a result. Before you write this off as being too fanciful, consider the sense of pride that infuses Paul's words as he starts his first letter to the Thessalonian church: 'You became imitators of us and of the Lord... And so you became a model to all the believers.'[4]

Of course, our children develop characteristics by copying their parents and, if they have them, their older brothers and sisters. We smile as the youngest child attempts to repeat the behaviour of the older ones. Initially they do so inaccurately or in the wrong context, but over time they develop the same facility; indeed, they may overtake their older siblings and become more capable than them in some areas. At the age of two or three, my daughter used to pretend to read books as she copied her older (and therefore heroic) brother, who was starting to read for himself. Reading and writing, though,

---

[4]   1 Thessalonians 1:6–7

seem to be her 'thing', and now, at the age of six, she has already surpassed him. There is something in her that just seems to 'get' reading.

In our own children we see the relationship of nature and nurture played out. When the two influences work in harmony and in the right direction, we celebrate. Yesterday afternoon I asked Zoë what she wanted to be when she grows up. She gave it some thought, as if for the first time, and then stated that she would like to be a writer—which of course made me smile. She then went on, saying that if she couldn't be a writer she would be either a dolphin trainer or a teacher. I told her that I thought she would be a good teacher, and that I thought it was possible for her to be both a writer and a teacher if she wanted to, automatically encouraging the qualities I saw in her that I'd love to see her develop. Then Jed piped up, saying that he wanted to be a dolphin trainer too, which just goes to show how that no matter how much we accentuate a particular quality, our children may sometimes choose the ones we would reject.

As Paul explained, God loves us to 'be imitators of God… as dearly loved children'[5] and also to be imitators of our eldest sibling, Jesus, and the older Christians around us. He has a clear belief that nurture is significant in our development. He also recognises that sometimes nurture has to battle nature: we need to work to eliminate or control some of the elements within us that do not come from God. Just as my children have an unaccountable need to spend a portion of each day winding each other up, so we all seem to have within us a force that runs counter to the wishes of God.[6]

---

[5]   Ephesians 5:1
[6]   Galatians 5:17

I wonder if God looks at us sometimes, mystified as our selfishness leads us to act in wholly inappropriate, sometimes destructive or self-harming ways, and thinks, 'Where did all that come from?'

For now, however, let's focus on the positive and look for the characteristics that he does wish to see grow—the qualities that are wired into us, and those that we need to work to develop. Fortunately for us, false modesty is not one of them, and, as God is not British, he has written them down.

Unconditional love

Where love rules, there is no will to power; and where power predominates, there love is lacking. The one is the shadow of the other.
Carl Jung

You do not have to deserve your mother's love. You have to deserve your father's. He's more particular.
Robert Frost

Do I love my children? Of course. Do they know that? I hope so. But do they think there are times when I love them more than at other times? Possibly. So could it be that I inadvertently use love as a control mechanism, giving my children the impression that it is withdrawn when I disapprove of their behaviour?

Of all of the characteristics of God, unconditional love is perhaps the one that we find hardest to understand fully, because perhaps we have never really experienced it. If you are an oldest child, you may have a personality type that some of the psychologists of the Tavistock Institute call 'hold-up'. You may have learnt over time that the way to earn your parents' approval, and therefore love, was to eat all your greens, to do your homework, to perform well at sport, to be polite to visitors, to pass exams or exhibit any one of a million small performance indicators. They will never have explicitly said so. In fact, your parents may have actually said to you, 'We love you however well you do', but as children we were especially attuned to seeing them swell with pride when we did well. We were perhaps rewarded with extra pocket money or special gifts when we achieved.

The other side of the coin is that while our parents may never have told us that they actually disliked us when we performed badly, we can all remember moments when we embarrassed them with our failures or our poor behaviour. It would be a perfect display of control if a parent managed never to shout at a child who was rude to a neighbour. If you are of a similar age to me, you may have earned sufficient disapproval to have been sent to your room, to have been smacked, to have been told to 'get out of my sight' and not to come back downstairs until 'you have learnt to behave'.

If you have siblings, especially older brothers or sisters, you will know what it is like to be compared to them and, on occasion, come off poorly in the comparison. Once again, we know that most parents try never to make this assessment explicit but, if one child excels or is especially talented, the praise heaped upon them will be noticed especially by their sibling rivals. It might seem only natural to feel that another child is getting more love.

As I write this, I feel a small surge of embarrassment as I recognise my own shortcomings as a parent. I am pretty sure that I run the risk of communicating conditional love to my children a lot of the time, even though I don't think of it that way. It's just that it is easier to express love when my children are being communicative or well-behaved or cooperative. It is much harder, and perhaps therefore much more meaningful, to express love when the object of our love clearly doesn't deserve it.

If we are on the receiving end, so attuned are we to the concept of conditional love that we may often mistake an expression of undeserved love as an attempt to coerce or patronise us. Those who have experienced especially warped relationships in their past may believe that not only can love be earnt but that when they do receive love and affection, there is a price that must be paid, a service that must be given in return.

God understands that it is easy for us to love those who love us back,[7] but do we ever fully understand what it is to be loved unconditionally? Can I be the only person who fails to well up with gratitude, every time I am reminded that Jesus laid down his life for me even though I did not deserve it? Am I the only one who hears that even if I were the only sinner in the world, he would still have taken my punishment for me, and feels in response that I must do better, work harder, pray more, give more, be more, somehow to deserve the gift better? It is not that I feel especially unworthy, but I have been trained to write a 'thank you' note in response to every gift; I have been told so many times that I am lucky; I am programmed to believe that one good turn deserves another. As a consequence, I find myself searching for the appropriate response to Jesus' sacrifice of his life for me, and I just can't think what I can do.

There is a rather neat but entirely unhelpful phrase that

[7]   Matthew 5:43–46

I have heard a few times: 'Nothing you can do can make God love you any more, and nothing you can do can make him love you any less.' It perfectly sums up the notion of unconditional love, but gives me no help in understanding how I might respond. I am simply not capable of grasping the concept easily. Perhaps the only way is to try to put myself in God's place. The closest I can get to experiencing that type of love is to consider how I feel about my children. My behaviour, my parenting skills and my lack of control over my temper may lead me to communicate love to my children poorly, but the fact that I love them is not in question.

‡

Chapter Three

Joy

Feeling his pleasure

Seize from every moment its unique novelty and do not prepare your joys.

André Gide

Standing with my feet in the cold water as it surged and subsided, and looking back up the beach, I could see two figures approaching us, whirling along in a loose jumble of arms and legs across a couple of hundred yards or so of firm gold-brown sand. The sea was out as far as it could go, leaving behind a wide and perfectly flat expanse, which meant that it was a five-minute walk from the towels and bags we had left on the softer sand, up above the high-tide mark, to the sea itself. Dave and I had strolled down there, enjoying the fresh breeze that brought us some relief from the heat of the day. Turning to look back, I could see Joshua and Charlotte coming to join us—their chosen method of travel, the cartwheel. Hands over feet over hands over feet over hands, laughing and racing and tumbling; two small bodies in swimsuits. It was a perfect picture of childhood, and I smiled a smile of deep and peaceful contentment.

They had hardly chosen the most efficient method to come down the beach, and the cartwheels were not perfectly performed; they were just expressing themselves in their youthful vigour, spinning across the sand for no other reason than that they could, and somehow the freedom of the wide open space invited it. The memory still makes me smile: it is a cherished moment of pure delight in my children.

I wonder if I ever make God feel like that. I wonder if, by simply enjoying who I am and where I happen to be, in an expression that has absolutely no purpose or point, I somehow give God the same glow. I wonder if I am ever able to stretch out my physical and metaphorical limbs so freely and innocently and just be me. Surely, if I ever do, God must look at me and take pleasure in seeing me enjoy being the very person he planned me to be. Didn't he make me this way?

I ask these questions because, if I try to think about how I might bring my heavenly Father some pleasure, I don't usually come up with the idea that I should go and enjoy myself. Instead, I think about doing a bit more Bible reading, volunteering for a bit more service, praying a bit more, and generally being good—or I even think of stern words like 'commitment' and 'obedience'. We will deal with some of those later but, for now, let's concentrate on having some fun.

Of course, not everything that my children call 'fun' fills me with delight or even a warm glow, so what was it about this beach scene that struck such a perfect chord within? I think the fact that it took place in that wide expanse was significant. It spoke to me of freedom, of a lack of constraint, of possibility and potential. I just love the idea that my children feel fresh air and space and respond to it, that they have room to move and run and jump and spin. As I think about it, I visualise them rolling down a grassy bank as it stretches out in front of them, or racing through waist-high grass, or kicking leaves and stamping in puddles, and the mental images or memories force an involuntary smile. There is no doubt that children were made for space. When constrained, they can become greyer, less joyful beings.

Were we not all created for freedom and expression? When Jesus used a child as a metaphor to explain the type of people with whom he wants to share heaven,[1] was he hinting at something like this?

Yet, in my recent attempts to please God, I feel more as though I have been constraining myself. When I go to church I feel constrained by the social norms of the service and find it hard to picture myself running free. Even more constraining are my attempts to squeeze service time into my diary. I've read *The Purpose Driven Life* by Rick Warren[2] and found it extremely valuable. As I mentioned earlier, I've drafted a Life Purpose Statement and, in an attempt to live it, I find time every Friday morning to review my diary and look for evidence that I am living according to my primary and secondary callings. It's an attempt to have my life reflect my correct priorities, but it frequently manifests itself in more constraints and restrictions: 'If I move my time spent with my wife to Thursday evening, that will leave Wednesday evening to attend the men's meeting at church and I can still squeeze in an hour of private Bible study on Saturday evening.' It's as if I am trying too hard. The week ahead never feels like a wide open expanse of time in which to express myself, rather a labyrinth of commitments that I must negotiate my way through.

---

[1]   Matthew 18:2–4

[2]   Zondervan, 2003. I have also found *Growing Leaders: Reflections on Leadership, Life and Jesus* by James Lawrence (BRF, 2004) very helpful.

Uncomplicated

When the solution is simple, God is answering.
Albert Einstein

Back on the beach, I remember turning to Dave, seeing the same smile of recognition on his face and commenting, 'This is how childhood should be.'

When you think about your children (if you have any), what sort of childhood do you want for them? If you looked in the three bedrooms upstairs in our house, at the piles of primary-coloured plastic, the battery-powered electronic gadgets, the books and the toys, you'd be forgiven for thinking that I was trying to hide my children behind the clutter. Can I be the only father who feels that all of this stuff is wrong? In fact, I know I am not, because when I talk about great childhood experiences with my contemporaries, we never ever discuss that fantastic day when I got another game for my Nintendo DS. Of course, we didn't have such things, and I can't shake off the feeling that we were richer for the lack.

Before I descend into a Werther's Original-fuelled reminiscence about the 'good old days', perhaps I should draw myself back to the present and consider what it is that fills me with joy about my children now. Inevitably, because of the availability of technology, the disposable nature of our society, the improvements in material living standards and the sheer explosion of opportunity that modernity offers most of us in the developed world, our lives are filled with greater complexity. Where children's TV used to squeeze in between the arrival home from school and the early evening news, children now have several dedicated channels broadcasting all day. Where the screen used to show just broadcast media, it now offers games, the internet, DVDs—and who knows what else in the coming years. Children now can attend after-school clubs and circus skills courses and skate parks and more.

Adult life is similarly complex. As I type right now, it is 9.42 on a Sunday evening, but lying next to the laptop is a BlackBerry, ready to provide me with several forms of communication to almost anywhere in the world instantly. My dad used to come home from work for lunch, and now I carry work with me wherever I go.

I don't really want to return to the days when the Etch-a-Sketch was cutting-edge handheld technology, though! In fact, I think that much of this stuff, and all of these opportunities, are wonderful and I don't really bemoan any of them. It's just that I still have this feeling of disquiet, as though amid the electronic noise I am missing something, as though we are all being distracted. With the brilliance of the toys, the beautiful design of the interfaces, the lights and the buzzers and the bells, I find my attention drawn to the toys and technology, and it is fun. Out on that broad beach, though, my focus was on the children and I felt more than fun—I felt joy.

On our fridge we have a jumble of pictures held in place precariously by magnets. One is of my two youngest children, covered in dust and dirt at the bottom of a concrete tube that used to run down from the back of our house in Nepal. The polished concrete was their slide, and they spent many hours shuffling down it on the seat of their trousers, bits of cardboard, scraps of carpet and slivers of wood. Next to that photo is a picture of them both sitting in the oversized washing bowl that we had to use for a bath in our house in Nepal. Another shows Zoë sitting on our front door step, gripping a small kitten slightly too tightly. I love all of those images because they focus on the children themselves. Early this afternoon, my eldest son wanted me to come and watch what progress he had made on his mountain board, so I stood for two hours on the top of a windy Cheshire hill and watched him hurtle down a steep grassy slope and up a ramp as he 'pulled an indie'. I loved that too.

You see, I love my children. Even more, I love to watch them showing off to me what they can do, be it reciting the proper names of dinosaurs, playing the James Bond theme on a guitar, or even mastering a new move on the Wii fit-board. I love it when I see what they can do—and, even more, when they see what they can do, when they express their identities for no other reason than for the joy of it.

We know that God takes delight in us.[3] In fact, he takes delight in us especially as humble beings, creatures of limited merit in comparison to him. He sees our potential and knows that, while it is good, it is nowhere near his, but he still enjoys watching us stretch out and exert ourselves in a simple celebration of what we are and what we can do. Yet, somewhere along the line I feel as though I have made pleasing God a duty. It is almost as if I have become my own Pharisee, a modern-day personal equivalent of those guardians of Jewish law, and Jesus' least favourite acquaintances—burdening myself with rules and requirements. If I can just get through the day without making a mistake, then perhaps I will feel as though I have made God happy—but I never do. For me today, Joshua's tumbles from the mountain board, the way he brushed off failure lightly and still wanted to give it another go, gave me as much pleasure as his eventual successes; and I returned home as desperate as he was to show my wife the photograph of all four wheels off the ground as he finally

---

[3]   Psalm 149:4

landed a jump. You see, I'm even boasting to you about it now. He came home grubby but exultant. It was great.

Jesus told people that it was not their rule-keeping that delighted God.[4] He may well keep a record of our lives, but I don't think that record is the list of errors that crops up in jokes about the pearly gates. I think it is more like the photo album that we keep of our kids, full of moments of achievement and fun and laughter. The archangel Michael may have my name in his register,[5] but God has a dog-eared bundle of well-thumbed snapshots.

Learning to cartwheel

I've been a missionary and I'm certainly not one to shy away from the importance of purpose, but I do believe that we have become too obsessed with right living as a way to please God. We set standards we can't keep: we talk on Sunday about ways to behave that don't conform to the behaviour of society around us, but by Tuesday our weakness and our need to fit in make us painfully aware of our inability to live up to our own rhetoric. All the time, God wants us to be free.

I think we should show off a little more to God.

The coming day, or the year, or the rest of our lives can stretch out before us like a maze of corridors interspersed with junctions and doors leading into yet more passages. The journey through the labyrinth can feel like a series of forced choices—some good, some bad, some mundane and others crucial—and perhaps it is tempting to think of God's

---

[4]   Mark 7:5–7
[5]   Daniel 12:1

plan for our life[6] as being something like that. But is that how you would map out the future for your children? I think I'd like to stretch out a blank canvas for them—a wide, flat beach—and I'd like them to determine their own path, whether they run straight, jump sideways, skip towards the rocks, clamber through pools, or get sand in their hair. Then, when they eventually choose to cartwheel towards me, I'll know it was an option that they chose. More than that, they will have done so in a way that allowed them to express themselves and develop a greater understanding of their own personalities and capabilities. Perhaps my joy will be deeper because I know that the person they have become, the person who chose to race towards me, is a cocktail in which some of the ingredients are mine but others are entirely theirs.

This all makes me wonder. I don't believe that God finds joy in constraining us. We like to characterise various pivotal moments in life as like being at a crossroads, and many times I have agonised over deciding whether left is good and right is bad. But perhaps the ultimate father prefers unencumbered children. I am going to resolve to find the things I am good at, the things that I love to do, the characteristics that my Father gave me, and I am going to do them more. I think he made me to do them, and I think that when I do, he smiles.

---

[6]   Psalm 139:16

Chapter Four

Peace

Peace that passes all understanding

To me, faith means not worrying.

John Dewey

Wouldn't you love to be able to sleep like a child? Our youngest will often fall asleep on our bed on a non-school evening and, before I can get settled, I have to pick him up and carry him through to his own bed. When I do, he perfectly communicates the concept of dead weight, his body free of any tension whatsoever. His face relaxes in that gummy, open-mouthed way that suggests he has only the very weakest possible grip on the saliva gathering in one cheek. I've been known to bounce his head off the wall accidentally without disturbing him. It can't be anything to do with being tired, though. I simply refuse to believe that he has yet plumbed the depths of tiredness that I have known as a working parent of three children, yet, if you tried to pick me up, drag me into another room and dump me down unceremoniously, I suspect you might get more of a reaction from me (not to mention a hernia).

For me, one of the few things I miss about the first year of each of my children's lives is that they now rarely, if ever, fall asleep while I am carrying them. To be walking along with a baby and to watch as its eyelids finally lose the fight against gravity, to feel the way they suddenly get that little bit heavier on your shoulder, to hear the slow regular breathing and smell the sweet milky breath, is a joy like no other. I know that part of this feeling is a sense of relief, because it means that for at least the next two hours they will not be crying or demanding, and that they are leaving me free to get some work done, have a quiet cup of tea, watch the TV or—oh sweet relief—grab a couple of hours of sofa-sleep myself. But the fact remains: when our children fell asleep on my wife's shoulder, I felt a twinge of jealousy because I just loved it when it was me who had rocked them off to sleep.

I have often said that having a baby fall asleep on you makes you a better person. I believe this is true, because it is the moment when you experience being utterly and completely trusted. Perhaps it happens because of a baby's inexperience of life—their utter naivety—perhaps because the idea that a parent may be fallible has not yet entered the consciousness of an infant. Whatever the reason, it is a moment to savour when a human being feels so safe with you, so completely comfortable in your embrace, so secure, that they fall into sleep and let you carry them where you will. Next time you get the chance, look closely at the face of a baby who has just succumbed to sleep on a parent's shoulder. I challenge you to find a better definition of peace. For those of you who have been fathers, I ask you to remember a moment when you were able to stop and gaze at the face of your child as they slept. Can you remember the thoughts and emotions that seeped into your consciousness in those contemplative moments? Can you recall the sense that some of the fundamentals of your relationship with your child were being reconfirmed? Did you, like me, silently rededicate yourself to care for your son or daughter to the very best of your abilities?

In those still moments, I found myself reminded of the incredible responsibility that I had in being a parent. I would see in my children's stillness a vulnerability that I found harder to recognise in their waking moments. I believe that God, as our parent, feels his own sense of responsibility to us even more keenly. Where are the moments in my life when I sink into his arms and rest as a peaceful and trusting child, accepting his enveloping protection, and, in resting, deepen my dependent relationship with him? My life, even my walk with God, seems to be characterised by frantic activity. Why do I never stop moving? I seem to have absorbed the idea that, as with my career, my advancement in the spiritual life depends on the hours I put in, the results I deliver, the lessons I have learned. If there were an annual review of my spiritual performance, I suspect that I would prepare for it by gathering evidence of how many hours I have spent in prayer, how often I have studied the Bible, how well I have completed the daily devotionals, how my church attendance record has been, and how much I have contributed to good causes. These are, of course, all good things (as I have said before) but I don't believe they are the things that matter most to God.

Right from the very beginning, as God laid out the foundations for the way in which his relationship with us should work, he instituted the concept of sabbath—rest. In the Old Testament it was a time for people to stop working for their food and to rest. In doing so, they were to rely not on the labour of their hands but on God's provision to get them through the day—or even the whole year.[1] Then, in the case of the year of Jubilee, it was a time to go back to their roots.[2] They might have spent 49 years toiling and building up possessions and slaves, taking rents and rearing flocks, but

---

[1]   Leviticus 25:1–7

[2]   Leviticus 25:13–23

in the 50th year all property was to be returned to its original owners, restored to where it started.

This astonishingly radical teaching was intended as a reminder that what God had given to the people at the beginning, as they entered the promised land, was enough. Although toil was important, ultimately everyone should return to the position in which they started, where all they had was a gift from God. They were brought back to trusting him to provide for their needs. Any benefits or advances that they could earn through the work of their own hands were necessarily temporary; anything of permanence or substance had already been given to them. As we consider the houses we have bought, the possessions we have accumulated, the fruits of our labours, that thought should be liberating. The sabbath is a time of rest, a time of trust, and a time to reassess the order of things, the priorities in life.

Our current interpretation of sabbath is as a day when we need to go to church and perhaps take the chance to spend time with our families, weed the garden, indulge in our preferred pastime or, more likely, drive our children to theirs. We may wish that shops were shut on Sundays or be grateful that the DIY superstore is open, and somehow, rather than seeking peace and a sense of dependence on God, we talk ourselves into believing that a change (in the type of frantic activity) is as good as a rest. It is not.

Practising peace

We are, perhaps uniquely among earth's creatures, the worrying animal. We worry away our lives, fearing the future, discontent with the present, unable to take in the idea of dying, unable to sit still.
Lewis Thomas

I want to be explicit: I am not suggesting that the way you or I organise our Sundays should necessarily change. This coming Sunday will see me spending some time with my children, driving one of them to gym training, rushing back to lead and speak at an evening service at our church, and finally getting home somewhere close to 8.00 p.m. It will be different from the way in which I spend the other days of the week. The focus will be on my family and on God. As I look forward to it, though, the words 'rest' and 'peace' do not readily spring to mind. I don't happen to think there is much wrong with that, and I am not going to beat myself up with guilt, thinking that somehow I should be so well organised that I can spend my day sitting still. In fact, I personally find periods of enforced stillness more exhausting than activity.

I am learning that peace and rest in the spiritual sense are about an adjustment in my understanding of trust and security. Just as I treasure those moments when my children slumped in my arms, allowing me to cradle them, so I believe God treasures those moments when we relax in his arms, recognising that there is no safer place to be. Freed from the misconception that everything relies on us, we can truly be at peace. These are moments that reassert who is the parent, who is the child, and who has the ultimate responsibility for safety and security. With those roles correctly established and reinforced, the relationship is deepened.

In my experience, dependence on God is most commonly discussed among men as a decision of last resort, when everything else has failed and when circumstances have forced us to a place where we have to turn to God. Like Job, or in the words of the Matt Redman song, we have to see all else stripped away before we simply come to God. But I would like to advocate an attempt to cultivate peace in our lives, not as an escape from turmoil but as a deepening of our relationship with our heavenly Father. I would like to recommend a regular practice of rest, but I'm not sure we necessarily need to sit still to do it.

I suggest that our sabbaths should be an adjustment of attitude, recognising that all we have and will have of substance comes from God. Try looking at the things you have that you truly value, or at the things that you believe would make a lasting improvement to your life. Don't feel you're being more holy by ignoring material possessions: God makes it clear that he recognises our need for food and clothes and shelter.[3] Having thought about all this, I want you to consider how God will provide these things for you. I'm not seeking to diminish the fact that you may work to earn money, but I'm asking you to go deeper and recognise where the talent and strength and resources that enable you to do the work ultimately come from, and to recognise that God has always planned to provide for you. That is his responsibility, which he gladly takes on. He would have you free from the burden of worry about such matters. Practise telling yourself that God does provide and will continue to do so. If meditation sounds like far too 'spiritual' a practice for you, just consider the words of the Lord's Prayer,[4] and try to live them. Ask God to give you your daily bread and free you from temptation. Trust me: there is peace and rest in giving him that responsibility. If he does not live up to his side of the bargain, you are free to get angry with him.

I'm not being flippant when I say that. It would be wrong to suggest that no Christian ever went hungry, that no Christian ever got sick or was poor or spent a night with-

---

[3]   Matthew 6:31–32
[4]   Matthew 6:9–13

out shelter or died. While true material poverty is relatively rare in 'developed' countries, many people all over the world go without. During my time working in Nepal, I met and got to know Christians facing genuine deprivation. My overwhelming experience was that these people had a much better understanding of peace, were much better at resting in the arms of God, than those of us who have better visible evidence of his provision. In fact, as I listened to the stories of believers who had suffered the ravages of leprosy and had, as a result, been cast out from families, cut off from inheritances and made to beg for food, I sensed that they had developed an acute understanding of their reliance on God for their daily needs; they simply had no other options. They had such a sense of peace that it was not uncommon for them actually to thank God for their afflictions, because the suffering had been instrumental in bringing them to meet with Jesus and recognise him as their Saviour. To me, a well-fed, well-educated Westerner, it was almost incomprehensible.

While God cares about our material needs, he also makes it clear that they are not the only or even the most important concerns, and that seeking him is the first priority.[5] For those who have developed the ability to be at peace about their material circumstances, a barrier seems to be removed. They become free to pursue the most important relationship of all, with the one whose love and resources are infinite. How peculiar, how typically counter-intuitive it is, that those who have so little are often able to trust God, to rest in his arms, far more easily than those who are surrounded by abundance. My advice to you, therefore, is to practise recognising the source of your material security, to work actively on seeing

[5] Matthew 6:33

your heavenly Father as a provider of all you need. Don't go from there into an excess of gratitude, but instead say a simple 'thanks' and curl up in his arms as a well-fed child. Relax and find peace.

If you don't, he may have to resort to removing your precious security blanket of self-reliance, in which you put so much faith, just to get your attention. That will work too, but it's a good deal more painful!

Chapter Five

Patience

I'm waiting!

You can learn many things from children. How much patience you have, for instance.

Franklin P. Jones

Patience, we are told, is a virtue.[1] We like our children to develop patience. I'm tempted to say that, with time and experience, we develop more and more of it, but I'm not sure the evidence always bears that out. There have been all too many occasions when I've stood at the bottom of the stairs, keys in hand, urging my offspring to get their shoes on, grab their coats and stop messing about, because they are making us late. Frequently I am exasperated by their failure to do what I ask them to do, when I ask them to do it. I find it difficult to understand why they have to watch another 30 seconds of television when they have been told that their dinner is waiting on the table.

No, I guess I am not always a patient man—but I do like my children to be patient. For example, when I am talking on the phone about an important issue and one of them starts tugging at my trouser leg because they want me to come and look at something, or want a snack or any one of a countless

---

[1]   Galatians 5:22

number of petitions, I like them to be patient and polite and to wait until I have finished. They seem to find this lesson very hard to learn. Of course, if I was on the phone and they were alerting me to a genuine emergency, patience would not be required or appropriate. In those circumstances it would be right for them to come and find me, and I would drop the phone and come running. In fact, if they didn't break in on my conversation when an emergency had occurred, I would probably chasten them: 'Why didn't you interrupt me?'

As with so many matters, patience is about perception—or perhaps I should say that impatience is about relative perceptions. When my children come to me, their priorities are almost always radically different from mine or indeed most adults'. When my wife is busy with a task, perhaps preparing dinner, she is understandably dismissive of urgent childish requests to come and see something utterly hilarious that has just happened on television. If they ask her to come and see one of their drawings, however, she will normally explain that she just has to put down the hot dish she is holding before coming to see their creation. The children's pleading may be identical in both situations—in fact, they are aware that the drawing will not disappear but the television programme will soon be over, so the latter may be presented with greater urgency—but my wife holds clearly formed views on the relative importance of the cooking, the drawing and the TV programme.

In the case of the cooking, the importance is clear. Food is important, and a hot dish left in a precarious position is even more so. Naturally my wife judges that safety comes first, not least because it is far more likely that one of the children would be the victim of a falling casserole than she. Of course, magnificent as my wife is (and more of that later), she is not perfect and there are occasions when she may actually be thinking that all she wants is a break from the children or to make sure the kitchen worktop does not get singed, but let's ignore that for now. She may also judge, though, that coming to see a drawing is important enough to delay the preparation of dinner. Not for one moment does she think that art is more vital to her children than food, but delaying dinner for 20 minutes is a small price to pay for encouraging creativity. So, wiping her hands on the tea towel, she will admire the barely discernible dinosaur as if it is the founding work of a whole new artistic genre, discussing it with the artist in some depth. If she and the artist agree, it may be displayed on the fridge or the wall, and our little Picasso will seize another piece of paper and start on a new masterpiece.

What the children may not understand is why their mother is so much less interested in coming to share the joke in the TV cartoon. They are clearly getting just as much fun out of it, but she is not persuaded by their urging to come and see. Of course, to watch it would only delay the meal by five minutes: she is a woman, after all, and therefore immune to the strange force that the TV exerts over men, whereby its very presence in the room, no matter how puerile the broadcast, is enough to hold our rapt attention for hours. No matter how hard they push, her resistance is not about her need to get her objective achieved. If it were, she would be more likely to spend five minutes watching the programme than 20 minutes cooing over the drawing. She is, in fact, communicating to our children what she considers to be the correct relative priority both for her and, more importantly, for them. She is teaching them. It's not deliberate; there is no lesson plan; it's just that my wife (who is instinctively one of the best parents I have ever seen) senses that she should be communicating an awareness of right priorities. It's OK to watch children's cartoons (if it wasn't, she would turn the

TV off), but developing creativity and meeting basic needs for food and safety are far more important.

The crucial point here is that we see someone as impatient when we think they have got their priorities wrong. We want our children to develop patience because it is a sign that they are learning what is genuinely most important, even though the immediacy of some of their desires may lead them in different directions. My wife does this stuff very well. How much better, then, does a perfect Father do it?

Quick stop, slow go

Patience and perseverance have a magical effect before which difficulties disappear and obstacles vanish.
John Quincy Adams

I find it difficult to imagine that God wants us to learn patience because he prefers people who spend most of their time sitting and waiting. It is hard to believe that David spent most of his time just sitting on his hands: surely someone who, as little more than a child, approached the king, pushed past the grown-up soldiers and insisted that, although he hadn't yet grown into the armour, he should nonetheless be the champion of his nation was not someone who found it easy to cool his heels. Peter rushed over the lake to meet Jesus, Moses set off alone up a mountain, Joseph took on the administrative responsibility for a whole foreign nation, and Esther risked death for her people; none of them sound like people who just hung around idly waiting for the solution to their problems to appear. They had to be patient, of course. It took some time for David to become king, Moses found himself in the wilderness enduring a time of preparation for leadership, and Joseph had to languish in jail for years. I don't know if they were at peace as they endured these delays but I also don't believe that they were characters who let life just happen to them. I cannot imagine the jailer handing over responsibility to Joseph because he sat in a shady corner looking serene.

I don't believe at all that God wants us to be passive, any more than I want my children to sit on the sidelines waiting for life to come to them. At the same time, I don't want the lives of my children—or, for that matter, my own life—to be characterised by impatience, by a finger-drumming, foot-tapping sense that things are moving just a little too slowly for their liking.

We most often think about developing patience in response to unanswered prayers. I want my friend to become a Christian now; I want another friend to be healed; I want yet another to be reconciled to his wife, and still another to be freed from an addiction. For myself, I have other wants. I want to be a better husband; I want to be a better father; I want to eliminate my own weaknesses; I want to understand better what God wants for my life; I want to know if I should take the job on offer to me. In some cases I've been brought to tears of frustration when faced with a dilemma, having asked for God to speak into the situation, only to hear a long-drawn-out silence or, at best, just static.

None of these petitions seem bad to me. I nearly always know when I am asking for something bad. In fact, even before I ask, I know that it's bad. The 'no' from my conscience comes to me even before I have framed the question. If my children ask my wife whether they can watch a film that she judges is too old for them, they don't need patience to wait for the answer; it tends to come pretty quickly. They may need to learn obedience but not patience.

Let's pause to consider what lies behind this scenario. I wish I could list the number of times my Christian friends have spoken to me about facing two options and feeling frustrated by God's apparent lack of response to their request for guidance. I've done it myself, and perhaps you have too. What has been my response to the silence? I've asked God for the same guidance again, and again, and again, and again. My friends have sympathised with my waiting and have even commended my persistence in prayer. Strangely, though, the waiting and the praying have rarely produced in me a quiet acceptance, but rather a growing frustration and disappointment that I can't hear God's voice for some reason. In such fertile territory the seeds of doubt and confusion and worry sprout, and, if not nipped in the bud, they become thorny, entangling bushes. Can that be what God means by patient endurance? Learning to live with the disappointment of not hearing him, all the while battling the weeds of doubt and insecurity? That doesn't sound to me like the approach of a perfect Father.

So, if a human parent quickly moves to rule out anything that is clearly bad for us, what are we to think about those times when we are repeatedly tugging at God's trouser leg? Logically, if we are not hearing a clear 'no', perhaps we should conclude that our request is not inherently bad. Within this conclusion are (at least) three assumptions. Ignoring the silly questions that doubt his very existence ('Does God actually hear me or is he too preoccupied by other stuff?' and so on), I am assuming, first of all, that God's concern is about what is best for me. If I regard him as a perfect Father, that does not seem like an outrageous supposition. The second assumption is that he actually knows what is best for me. Again, bearing in mind that he created me, created the universe and exists outside the constraints of time, perhaps we can regard this as a given. Thirdly, and perhaps more controversially, I am assuming that when I start to consider a course of action that is bad for me, before I have even formed the question,[2] God will speak clearly enough to let me know the error.

When I think something is wrong or dangerous for my children, I make it as clear as I can. I stop what I am doing, I crouch down so that my face is level with theirs, I look them in the eye and check they are giving me their full attention, and I speak slowly and clearly. Sometimes I explain the reason why, and sometimes, because I fear that the horror of the consequences may be too much for them, I simply tell them that I have their interests at heart and ask them to trust me. Whatever I do, I make sure that I have told them, and that they have heard and understood. It is in the character of God to do the same, for some issues by means of the pricking of our conscience, and, for the really crucial issues, through very explicit scriptural prohibitions.[3] Imagine the conversation:

'God, I'm thinking of sleeping with my friend's wife.'

'No.'

'Well, OK, but can I just tell a small lie?'

'No.'

'All right, but a little stealing?'

'Nope.'

'Some murder, then?'

'Watch my lips. No.'

Some of the Bible is allegorical; some of it is tricky to understand because the nuances do not neatly cross language and cultural divides; other parts are clearly specific to particular times and societies, and we may struggle to apply

---

[2]   Psalm 139:4

[3]   Exodus 20:13–17

them to our lives today. But when God wants to make clear what is wrong, he seems more than capable of expressing that command unambiguously. Like an errant child, we may choose to disobey or we may think that we know better, but it does not seem to be in his nature to leave us in any significant doubt. Clearly we don't need patience to discern right from wrong.

So if you are waiting for God to respond to your question about which of two options is the wrong one, his silence is the answer: neither. As Jesus himself taught, does it seem likely that a human father would present his child with two baskets, one of which contains an egg and the other a scorpion, and watch the child agonise over which one to choose?[4] Why do we fear that God might be less, not more, concerned for our well-being?

All of this means that we do not have to wait patiently when we ask God for something that is wrong—only when we ask him for something that is right, but perhaps not as important as something else that he is doing or wanting for us. As a perfect parent, he is placing our well-being at the top of his priority list.

Patience and perspective

All wisdom can be stated in two lines:
'What is done for you—allow it to be done.
What you must do for yourself—make sure you do it.'
Ali al-Khawwas

---

[4] Luke 11:11–13

One of the key processes in growth is the expansion of our sphere of perspective. Babies know of nothing but their own physical sensations and needs. They experience hunger and fullness, discomfort and comfort. During their very earliest days, they don't even really know when you are with them, their focus being constrained to a relatively short distance. A new mother has to come close to her child so that the baby can recognise her face.

Toddlers are certainly aware of much more, such as when their parents have left the room, but their world is still constrained to their own selfish desires. They don't understand how their demands affect a tired parent or an irritated older sibling. They simply know what they want and complain when they don't get it. In time, they learn that there are wider issues than their own concerns and more going on in the world than whatever directly and immediately impinges upon them. We may have to reach adulthood before we start to comprehend that our choices and actions have implications that spread outside our own house, street, town and even country. Our consumption choices and votes mingle with those of other people to have an impact on our entire world: although we may feel powerless, we are far from it.

God tells us that our choices go even further than this. He makes it clear that we are spiritual beings and that our actions resonate throughout a realm that we rarely perceive. Sometimes we are a little like toddlers ourselves, making demands of a heavenly parent, ignorant of the longer-term and wider implications. Like any parent of a toddler, God wants to see us develop some patience. As I have suggested, though, this patience does not imply just sitting and waiting for God to act. Rather, he is looking for us to develop an acceptance that he knows what is best for us, that we can rely on his judgment. When we don't get the response we expect or the immediate answers we demand, he wants us to develop enough imagination to realise that there will be a reason for it. What is more, that reason will not be about God's capacity to respond, but will relate to our own safety and development. In short, like any parent, God sees in our patience our recognition of his priorities.

Precisely because our perception of time and of the spiritual realm that God chiefly inhabits is so poor, our patience must be rooted entirely in our trust in God rather than an understanding of what he is doing. When we give our babies their first inoculations, we don't even bother trying to explain to them what we are doing or why. Even though it hurts, even though it makes them cry, precisely because the children have learnt over days and weeks to trust their parents, they even turn to the parent for comfort.

Perhaps this is another interpretation of coming to God as a little child. Let's take a look at the Bible character who most famously and repeatedly badgers God for an explanation: Job. If we also look at God's response to him, we find that it's prefaced by a promise that Job is about to learn some wisdom.[5] God himself has to show some patience as the last of Job's companions talks on and on, and eventually, to get some attention, God raises his voice.[6] When he does, though, he offers no explanation for his actions whatsoever—no justification or excuses, no attempt to help Job understand what is being achieved through his suffering. Remember, Job's experience is not actually about him at all. It is about something well outside human understanding—an object

[5]   Job 33:31–33

[6]   Job 38:1–3

lesson for Satan, arranged by God.[7] Perhaps God could have explained to Job that he had a crucial role as a pawn in a spiritual debate. Perhaps he could have explained how he had plans to prosper Job in the long term. Perhaps he could have asked Job to be patient for a while and endure so that he might reward him later, showing him a glimpse of a greater prize to come. Why didn't he do that?

The human response to someone who is clearly struggling is normally just that—to point out that it will come good in the end. How often do we try to comfort others by explaining that God's plans will make everything much better in future?[8] Does it work? When you are in despair, how successfully does that promise lift you? Not a great deal, because the people who quote those verses from Jeremiah conveniently neglect to mention that the recipients of the promise were warned that they would have to wait 70 years in exile before they would see its fulfilment. To put it another way, all those old enough to understand the promise were likely to be dead before it was fulfilled. That is perhaps about as comforting as explaining to a baby that the pain from the needle is worth enduring because he will not be getting mumps some 17 years later, when the baby has no concept either of mumps or of a single week, let alone 17 years. So when God asks the exiles or Job to show patience, he is not asking them to wait for the answer to come.

God does not bother with an explanation to Job. Instead he makes clear why, despite the immediate evidence, he is worthy of trust. He shows Job that he has everything under control.[9] In listing his own responsibilities and actions, God

---

[7]   Job 1:6–12

[8]   Jeremiah 29:10–11

[9]   Job 38:4–41

shows that the depth of his knowledge, the breadth of his understanding and the all-encompassing nature of his work dwarf the limited perception of any single human being. He says, 'Trust me, because in reality you have no other choice; to doubt me is to display only your ignorance of all that I am doing.' He asks for patience, not because a better day is coming, not because there is a reward on offer, and not even because it makes sense. He asks for patience as a sign that we know we can trust him with the circumstances we can see and, even more so, with those we cannot understand.

Chapter Six

Kindness

Sibling rivalry

Be kind, for everyone you meet is fighting a hard battle.
Plato

The other day, my eldest son, Joshua, was attempting to raise some money for his gymnastics club through sponsorship. I should perhaps explain that this was not just another one in the seemingly endless round of sponsored fundraising events heralded by a child returning from school and thrusting a photocopied grid at parents and grandparents, who are urged to offer a handful of pence in return for a stroll around the running track or half an hour of skipping. For Joshua, life is divided into four distinct categories, which I list here in order of decreasing delight:

1. Doing gymnastics
2. Travelling to gymnastics
3. Sleeping
4. Waiting until the next gymnastics training session

I'm afraid that everything else, including attendance at Sunday school and eating, falls a far distant second to his sport—and he is only eight years old. So, for Joshua, the chance to raise funds for the club was an evangelistic opportunity.

Younger sister Zoë understands just what this means to

Joshua, and so she asked to sponsor him. When we asked how much she would like to give, she offered all the money she had—some £18, the remains of her Christmas money and the pocket money she had saved up over the past few weeks. It was her version of the widow's mite,[1] postponing the purchase of more of the toy pet characters she is collecting assiduously. Of course, we talked it through and ensured that Zoë did not give all of her savings but, as proud parents, we felt a little thrill of pleasure at the selfless kindness she displayed.

This morning, however, the stuttering journey from waking to herding the children out of the door and off to school was regularly punctuated by my daughter's repeated attempts to wind up her brothers. Gone were any consideration or sensitivity, replaced by a need to see just how much of a reaction she could get from them, for no particular reason that I could discern. It was hard to reconcile her behaviour here with that of the generous child of the day before. Not for the first time, I wondered at the inconsistency of it all. What happens to them overnight? One moment they are a team, working and playing together, cooperative and considerate, and the next they are competing. For what? The complaints that accompany the altercations most frequently are not about concrete items but about relativity: the issue is not whether they get a sweet, some attention, a slice of cake or time on the Wii; it is whether the others are getting more sweets, attention, cake and game time. They most typically whine about injustice: 'It's not fair!'

It is certainly not that our children are being cruel to be kind, and their arguments are usually about the fact that,

---

[1]   Mark 12:41–44

from a childish perspective, things rarely seem to come in the right measure. As I watch these interactions, I notice that the issues children bicker about most of the time fall into two categories. Sometimes they argue about finite items, such a pile of biscuits to be shared, turns on a computer game before bedtime or which DVD they would prefer to watch, in which case the objects involved are almost always trivial, temporary and easily replaced or reproduced. On these occasions my wife and I find ourselves saying something like, 'Oh, for goodness' sake, it's only a slice of pizza. Yesterday you told me you didn't like pizza.' Or perhaps we just tut, sigh and shake our heads at the way a quarrel so irrelevant can cause so much emotional expenditure. Even more frustrating, though, are the times when they compete over things that are not limited. They fight for attention or love, failing to understand that the amount given to one has absolutely no impact on the amount available for another.

Of course, this kind of conflict is not about pizza and it is not about love. It is not even necessarily about injustice; above all, it is about winning.

Human racing

One can see the respect God has for riches by the people he gives them to.
Alexander Pope

One of the most persuasive arguments for the process of evolution is the fact that many of us behave much of the time as if we are programmed to believe in the survival of the fittest. So much of our life, and especially our emotional state, seems to be about competition. We can't help but notice that he has a better job, we have more money, they have better holidays and she is better dressed. Strangely, the clothes she wears have no impact on the clothes we can afford or choose to buy. There is clearly not just one BMW in the world, so, when he buys one, why do I feel poorer for it? When our neighbours show me the photographs of their camping holiday in Wales, why does the mention of a fortnight in Barbados feel like one-upmanship? Something inside us seems programmed to compete; something makes us feel that we must climb a little higher, as if there is a cost to being closer to the bottom.

The most obvious way to get to the top is to work hard, committing time and sweat to accumulating the trappings of success. The easier alternative would be to cheat or steal from others; when that does not seem an appropriate course of action, then damaging or destroying someone else's achievements is another way to advance—relatively speaking, that is. In a culture where doing such things physically is illegal, we can still use words. The human heart seems predisposed to ruthless striving against possible rivals, even when competition is completely unnecessary for survival.

Does God watch this competitive scrabbling around with the same exasperation that a parent feels, watching the irrelevant, irritating squabbles of childhood? Does he sigh, tut and wonder why we don't understand that if we all share, if we live lives of kindness rather than competition, everyone will be happier and more fulfilled? Occasionally, when he can take no more, does he intervene, perhaps even snatching away the very objects we were battling over, to make the point that life is not all about mere 'stuff'?

I had a colleague who talked of an 'abundance mentality' as being important in daily life. When we were discussing the allocation of charitable funds to specific projects, he used to ask us to imagine that there was a limitless supply of money—an exercise that I found irritating in the extreme, partly because macro-economics was a key component of my Masters degree, and I know that the money supply is finite. (A good thing, too: if it weren't, we'd have the sort of inflation that would require us to take articulated lorries instead of wallets on shopping trips.) So it is hardly surprising that I might consider a pound coin you hold as one denied to me, unless I win it from you.

Perhaps, though, having an abundance mentality is not about that at all. When we read in the Bible that God controls limitless herds of cattle, and has resources of unending magnificence,[2] we are tempted to believe that some of that wealth might filter our way if we are deserving enough! But maybe the point is that everything we actually need is already there in abundance. I don't recall God promising us hard cash![3]

This view of abundance mentality makes me begin to think differently about kindness. If we are promised everything we need, surely anything that is limited in supply must be something that God considers a surplus or luxury. If we think kindness means giving no more than money to a worthy cause, or, worse, if we decide not to give because we can't afford it (or give grudgingly because we think we will in some way feel the lack),[4] it may be that God watches us with the same emotions as a parent seeing their well-fed children unwilling to share a bar of chocolate.

Surely the most fundamental gift of kindness is the action demonstrating that we've seen a need in another person's life and want (not feel obliged) to help. It is about understanding

---

[2]   Psalm 50:10

[3]   Luke 12:15

[4]   2 Corinthians 9:7

and sensitivity and response. It is not about giving something up (more of that later) but about showing that we see what is going on and intentionally deciding to get involved. By this interpretation, Zoë's offer of £18 was important not simply because it was all the money she had. She doesn't need her pocket money to live on: she gets pocket money because it's important for her to learn about managing money. We buy her food and clothes for her, honest! What touched me about Zoë's gift was not the amount of money, and not even her willingness to give it (she didn't really need it herself), but the fact that she understood what was important to her brother and wanted to get involved in his agenda. Do you feel kind when you toss some coins into a Styrofoam cup sitting in front of a bedraggled man slumped on the street? Have you wondered whether what he really wants is a chat?

Chapter Seven

Goodness

Damaged 'good'

Waste no more time arguing what a good man should be.
Be one.

Marcus Aurelius

'Hasn't she been good?'

I overheard this comment as I retrieved my case from the overhead locker and filed off the aircraft with my fellow passengers, trying to get some life back into legs that had been folded into an economy seat for the best part of eight hours. It was addressed to the parents of a toddler sitting in their bulkhead seats, patiently waiting for others to disembark before they attempted to assemble the jumble of belongings that form part of any long trip with small children. The parents offered tired smiles back to the elderly woman who had given them the compliment. They were clearly relieved that the plane journey was over, although they had yet to negotiate queuing for customs, baggage collection and the taxi journey to their hotel with a young girl who at that moment was slumped in open-mouthed slumber across their laps.

In this circumstance, what was meant by 'good'? The passenger was commenting on the fact that the child had not been especially noisy, had not cried and had slept for the 50 per cent of the journey that she had not been glued to the small screen. In effect, she had not been a nuisance or an inconvenience to her fellow passengers.

We've taken the word 'good' and watered it down, damaged our understanding of it with over-use and misuse. Good enough to eat. Good for nothing. Good job! Good as gold. Good girl. Good at sport. It has come to mean 'fit for purpose, competent, well behaved and sufficient'. No wonder we struggle to understand the word when it is applied to God. Is God fit for purpose, sufficient and competent? I certainly hope so. Is God well behaved? Almost certainly not! The Old Testament is rife with examples of God as a distinct inconvenience to a great many people. He has times when he is not quiet or polite, when he is more than happy to disturb. When we describe God as 'good', and when we seek to see the quality of goodness developed in our own lives, we are talking of a wholly (not to mention holy) different concept. In everyday language, when we apply the word 'good' to our children, we are not talking of anything even vaguely related to the biblical use of the term.

When God is described as 'good', the word speaks of his perfection, so perhaps for that very reason we find few opportunities to apply it accurately in our lives. When it is written of a human being, it is perhaps best used as an explanation of what we are not, often juxtaposed with our description as 'sinners'.[1] So when God asks to see goodness developed in our lives, does he mean that he wants to see us becoming more perfect? That seems both illogical and unattainable, especially given that perfection is an absolute term: you can't be a little bit perfect, become more perfect, or ask if one person is more perfect than another. Striving for

---

[1] Romans 5:7–9

perfection is something that athletes might talk about but, as it is quite impossible for us mortals to achieve, we can feel as though it is not worth all of the effort.

Try, try again

On the whole, human beings want to be good, but not too good, and not quite all of the time.

George Orwell

My children are not perfect. I don't believe and have never for one moment believed them to be so, not least because a fair bit of what has gone into the making of them is from me. How could they be? I know them pretty well, so I've seen on a daily basis a quantity of strong evidence to suggest that perfection is some way off—and, though the phrase sticks in my throat, I know that they do sin. I don't want to try to calculate the percentage of time they do the right thing as opposed to the alternative, even if I could, and I don't want to list the examples of their sin. In fact, I tend to do the opposite, especially when I am talking about them to colleagues or friends. Rather than digging up examples of where they have done wrong, I am more likely to work the conversation round to what they have done well, listing their achievements.

Our children may not be perfect—we may not even kid ourselves that they are—but that does not stop us wanting them to be. In fact, we are probably more concerned than they are about seeing them as perfect. Sometimes my children are so ready to accept that they made a mistake, and to shrug it off, that I find myself wanting to drag them back to the moment to make absolutely certain that they are feeling at least the merest hint of remorse. Not too much, of course. I don't want them lugging a heavy burden of guilt around with them. I just want to be sure they have understood that what they have done is wrong; I want to be sure they are actually sorry and that, if there is a lesson to be learnt, they have grasped it. Then I want them to move on.

I'm afraid, however, that sometimes, in trying to make them see the error of their ways, I've overdone it—perhaps shouted at them or kept on at them too long, often releasing my own stress about something unrelated in the process. I've quickly found myself regretting that as I reduce them to tears. Of course, that was not what I intended. What I really wanted was for them to apologise as if they understood what they had done wrong, and then leave it behind and move on. Children and guilt are just not designed to go together. It is to our collective shame that they frequently do.

Just as for our children, our journey towards goodness is not going to be achieved through a burden of guilt, and God would not have it so. Like any proud parent, he makes it quite clear that he does all he can to focus on the times when we make the right choices, and, although he can't actually forget it when we make mistakes, he makes a deliberate choice to focus on the positives. He certainly does not dwell on our errors, any more than a good parent will constantly dredge up past wrongs at every opportunity.[2] He wants to see us as good as we can be. Indeed, in providing the perfect scapegoat, God manipulated the events of history to substitute Christ for us, for this very purpose. We can choose to see this sacrifice as the removal of our sins, but we can also choose to see it as the means through which God could credit us with unblemished

---

[2] Hebrews 8:12

righteousness, making it possible for us to appear completely perfect in his eyes.[3]

Imagine, then, a situation in which your child seemed to be dragging around unresolved issues that they could not let go. What would you want them to do? Talk to you about it, perhaps? Then you could explain that the event was not important to you; that you were more interested in them than in the past misdemeanour; that you wanted to help them let it go. I've seen this sometimes in my own children, and had to learn a very important lesson from my wife in dealing with it. As a man, I seem programmed to solve issues, to take them head-on, so I want to go to my son and talk to him and work out the solution. My wife, being wiser in such matters, shows me that it is better to leave him initially and wait until the moment, sometimes days later, when he is ready to discuss the issues on his terms. To try sooner simply stirs up more anger and negativity.

Here, then, are clues to help us resolve the mystery of how God feels about us and our struggles towards goodness. He does not expect perfection from us but delights in the moments when we make the right choices and achieve our small victories. Those are the moments that he chooses to remember, that he celebrates, just as we attach important certificates and photographs to the fridge. For those of us who are tempted to see the ledger maintained in heaven as a record of wrongs, it can be difficult to see God as a proud father. It may be easier to see him as a taskmaster, expecting an impossible standard of perfection from us. I think it more likely, though, that he is a Father who understands our capabilities and limitations fully. Such a Father could never

---

[3] 2 Corinthians 5:21

be disappointed in us if we fail to achieve something that is, in any case, beyond our capacity; that would show a lack of imagination and understanding.

While parents try to dwell on the good, though, they may be forced to address the mistakes or the wrongdoing for the good of the child.[4] In our minds, confession seems to be linked with punishment and guilt, as if God requires the breaking of our spirits, as if he can only rebuild us when we have been fully crushed under the weight of self-doubt and self-loathing. The truth is that we need the release that confession brings, and God makes himself available to reflect with us on the times when we have not been good, to lance the boil of sin, release the poison that eats away at us and help us make another fresh start.[5]

Perhaps, if we could see the act of confession as a service that God performs for us, we might embrace it more readily and so come to understand his heart better. Perhaps, if we could see confession as a part of the path to goodness rather than a detour from it, as thirst-quenching refreshment rather than a bitter pill to be swallowed along with our pride, we would better welcome the forgiveness that God holds out to us and more easily shed the guilt. Confession may be a vital part of salvation because the very act is an acknowledgment of the fact that God is a Father who prefers to see us as good.

---

[4] Psalm 38:18
[5] Proverbs 28:13

✥

Chapter Eight

Faithfulness

Proximity

You see many stars in the sky at night, but not when the sun rises. Can you therefore say that there are no stars in the heavens during the day? Because you cannot find God in the days of your ignorance, say not that there is no God.

Sri Ramakrishna

I have unashamedly borrowed heavily from my personal experiences in this book, and of course I have to. In this journey of self-exploration, if my life truly offers me moments of insight into my relationship with God, then to do otherwise would be at best insincere. But I am also aware of a couple of dangers in this approach. The first is the temptation to believe that all of you reading this (I hope there are more than two, because one of you is my mother, and she is hardly the target audience) are likely to have similar experiences to mine, when your experience of parenting or of God may be very different. I've tried to deal with much of that in the chapter on good and bad fathers and unconditional love, but if that is still jangling your nerves, I apologise. The second danger is that, in choosing snapshots from my experience, I may be giving you an impression that my current family life is like something picture-perfect from Walton's Mountain. So it seems appropriate to share today's events with you.

I am writing this chapter while sitting in a plane, suspended somewhere over the Atlantic at the start of a business trip that will separate me from my family for eight days. (It is amazing how the power of a publishing deadline can keep me away from the films available on the seatback in front of my face.) As is usual on the occasions when such a trip is due, my children exhibited clear 'packing behaviour', as I call it. I've seen it many times before. It is their expression of dislike at my impending absence and the effect it will have on their routines, manifested in a mixture of clinginess and small signs of their disapproval. I also know that a perfect father would deal with this behaviour by sitting down with them and talking through their feelings, making sure they have no doubt that I intend to return and that I love them, and of course tolerating their tendency to push me away in denial and defence. That's easy to rationalise, sitting here with coffee on tap.

However, in the chaos of trying to leave the house while everyone was getting ready for school, and partly because I was feeling guilty about leaving my wife alone with them for a week, I tried to help with the pulling on of school uniforms before breakfast. With my head full of tasks I'd not managed to complete at the office, I encouraged Joshua out of bed.

'Will you help me put my clothes on, Dad?'

'Of course,' I agreed, even though I know that, when motivated, he is more than capable of dragging his clothes on by himself.

He kicked off his pyjamas, leaving them in a heap on the floor next to his school clothes, and looked at me with a little eight-year-old aggression.

'Right, I'll fold your pyjamas while you get some pants and socks.'

'You get them!' he spat at me. I ignored this.

'And look at your trousers. They're far too muddy; we're going to have to get some clean ones.'

'You get them.' Again, rudeness.

'Right, well, if you won't help, I don't see why I should. Get yourself dressed, then.'

I walked out of the room, partly in search of clean trousers but mainly to show my disapproval of his attitude. As I headed down the stairs, I could hear my wife, much more sensitive than I to the root cause of this display, heading into Joshua's room to cajole him along. By the time I had reached the bottom of the stairs, I was already annoyed with myself. Brilliant! The last couple of minutes together for more than a week and I was turning my back on one of the children. The ensuing quarter of an hour comprised an attempt by the other two to stop me leaving the house by clinging to my legs, and then a brief argument with my wife in the driveway about how I'd been insensitive to her earlier in the week. I hate being away from my family, and I'm pretty sure they don't like me going away, and we don't handle it very well.

But what is the alternative? How about being with my children constantly, going everywhere with them, doing everything with them, sitting next to them at school, joining in with all of their after-school clubs, going to Rainbows with Zoë, staying at pre-school with Jed and so on? For a moment, leave aside the practical point that I have to earn a living and write books and so on. There is a family in our church with children roughly the same age as mine, in which the father sold a successful business, made a lot of money and now no longer needs to work. In fact, I suspect that he could afford to employ people to do all the household chores, too. What if he decided instead to spend every waking moment with his children? Would that work?

Of course not. Firstly, they wouldn't want it, no matter how brilliant a father he is. Just last night, as I dropped Joshua off at his gymnastics club, conscious of the fact that I would be going away, I asked him if he would like me to come in and help coach, as I all too rarely do. However, he was pretty clear in stating his preference that I should simply come back at finishing time to take him home. Furthermore, I instinctively know that, as he gets older, it will be an important part of his development to do some of these things himself without having me around. I don't want to suffocate him, do I? If I did, I suspect it wouldn't be long before we both needed some counselling. And, do you know, when I read the Bible I realise that God knows this stuff, too.

Omnipresence

The nature of God is a circle of which the centre is everywhere and the circumference is nowhere.
Empedocles

How do you feel about the idea that God is always here? The fact that he is cannot be in doubt. A skim-read of Psalm 139 convinces us that even if we try to hide, we can't get away from him. I have to say, though, that whenever I read this passage carefully I often emerge with slightly mixed feelings. I am a (reasonably) mature Christian, so the idea of being, let's say, a teenager or even a grown man who cannot get some space from his father sounds a bit unhealthy. I instinctively feel that if I am always with my sons, I risk breeding dependent adults who will constantly be looking for someone to tell them what to do rather than developing their own judgments. Without me as a guide, they may find a substitute for me, seeking guidance from other places without the ability to discern for themselves what is right and what is wrong. When I read the Bible, though, I find a God who does let us make our own mistakes and who expects his maturing sons and daughters to be able to handle themselves a bit when it comes to the fight. Yes, his presence is always with us, but that does not mean he is with us in an interfering or overbearing way.

When he faced a severe test at the beginning of his ministry,[1] Jesus was weakened physically through fasting and was left to his own devices to take on the tempter. He was able to find the spiritual strength to win through and stand firm. Can you imagine how proud God was as he watched his Son taking on all that was thrown at him, knowing that lesser men would have crumbled? Standing alone in this way seemed to be, for Jesus, a vital part of his development, almost a rite of passage.

Was there also some risk involved? Did God breathe a sigh of relief that the test had been passed and his Son had come away unscathed? I like to think he did, because what sort of test would it have been with no chance of failure? This is why I reject the idea of a God who is always with me, in the sense of being right on top of me, telling me what to do at every step. That is not my experience of God and it is not the type of fathering I want from him, just as I know that this is not the sort of father I want to be.

John Eldredge, in his book *The Way of the Wild Heart*,[2] describes how adventure and risk are important parts of the process of raising kids. I'd recommend it to anyone thinking about the amount of rope they need to give their children, especially in these times when 'health and safety' seems to take precedence over health and vitality. I believe that God, the perfect parent, lets us take risks, encourages us to stand

---

[1]   Matthew 4:1–11

[2]   *The Way of the Wild Heart: A Map for the Masculine Journey* (Nelson, 2007)

on our own two feet, and allows us to stray to areas that stretch us and force us to grow and develop. God may not lead us into temptation[3] but he does permit us to wander into areas that take us to the limit—if only so that we know where the limit might be. So when God is deciding how much rope to give us, he will certainly give us enough to allow us into places where we need to flex our muscles, perhaps beyond what we thought they could endure, so that we even feel unsafe and exposed. If, whenever we are tested, we know with utter certainty that we will be OK, the risk is gone and with it the stress. Yet, in the design of human beings, stress is a vital component of growth.

I used to teach outdoor pursuits, including climbing. I must have encouraged over a thousand people of a variety of ages through the very first steps in abseiling, when they have to lean back, commit their weight to the rope, and trust. Those to whom this exercise comes easily end their small first descent with, if anything, a little disappointment that it was over so quickly, and the event is forgotten easily. There are those, however, who teeter on the edge. They will probably have witnessed countless others hang off the rope, and may believe 100 per cent that it will hold them, but when it comes to putting that belief on the line and hanging 50 feet above the ground, they freeze. With coaxing and encouragement, sometimes over 20 or 30 minutes, they almost always manage it, overcome their fears and learn something about themselves.

Don't we want those formative experiences for our children? We want them to experience perceived risk, to face that fear, to develop courage and to come through. If this is to

---

[3]   Matthew 6:13

work, they must have moments of doubt, even though we, the parent or the outdoor pursuits instructor, may know that our child or student is safe.

Just as we can novice climbers that the safety rope can carry weights of several times their own, so God tells us that we will never be broken.[4] To be all that we can be, however, we must go to places where we doubt that we will come through, where we fear that there is no safety net, where we are stripped of complacency and ambivalence, where we can believe that the way we face those pressures and fears really, really matters.

I believe that you will have moments in your life when you feel that God has abandoned you. I can think of times in my life when I doubted, when the cord that joined me to God felt more theoretical than actual, when I felt 1 was really on my own. When I have the luxury of looking back on those times, I also believe that they have been the greatest times of personal growth. I don't think God ever leaves me, but I do think that having the experience of times when I fear he is absent is vital for my growth. I think God needs me to come through that fire. I can only believe that my heavenly Father will catch me if I am actually falling.

Personality

You cannot develop a personality with physics alone; the rest of life must be worked in.

Richard Feynman

---

[4]   1 Corinthians 10:13

Over the last few days, I have found myself surrounded by men expecting the arrival of their first children. In chatting with them, the conversation has quickly strayed to sleepless nights, nappy changing, and the challenge of generally getting used to looking after someone utterly dependent. I have also had to confess that I can't get particularly excited about the first nine months or so, except those moments when the child falls asleep on my shoulder—I just can't get enough of that. What I do love, though, are the months between crawling and the approach of their second birthday, when they seem to develop so quickly, adding new skills and abilities and achievements daily, and beginning to express themselves. I love the evidence that they have a personality.

Of course, as they grow further, the existence of that independent personality will mean that we are challenged and questioned by our children. Where previously they explored the world by treating us like an infallible walking encyclopedia ('Why do mice like cheese… spiders have eight legs… bees sting… trees lose their leaves…?'), they quickly progress to questions that challenge our authority. The 'why' questions are increasingly demanding as our children seek to develop a worldview that is not necessarily in agreement with ours. 'Why do I have to go to bed so early when you get to stay up? Why is it OK for you to tell me to be quiet but not OK for me to tell you? Why is it wrong to lie but OK for you to tell me Father Christmas was real?'

We've already talked about the idea of over-parenting, that too much parenting might actually stifle our children's development. Perhaps we can speculate that one consequence of this would be children who become devoid of personality when their father is with them, ending up as unthinking extensions of his will. I want to emphasise that word 'unthinking', because I certainly don't want my children to become unthinking automata or mindless adherents to a series of rules.

I find in myself some of the debris of an upbringing in which I understood that adherence to rules was particularly important. It comes out most strongly when I hear myself telling my children to sit still at the dining table, when I know they just can't sit still for that long. As my wife reminds me, that mindset comes from my parents, and yet, if you push me for an explanation, I am not absolutely certain why immobility at the table should be such a crucial life skill. I certainly want my children to consider others and to behave in a way that does not cause offence in a restaurant, but why do I need them stationary in the privacy of my (and their) own home? I think it would be fair to say that I have become a table Pharisee.

God isn't just ambivalent to obsessive rule obeyers; he seems to want to correct and chide them, often quite harshly. On countless occasions Jesus showed utter contempt for those men of learning who knew in depth their culture's rules and their application, and he was especially condemning of those who decided that the way to control others was through prescriptive instruction and a finger ready to point out any transgressor. He didn't like the idea of control at all.

In consequence, both Jesus and his Father often chose to work with and through abrasive, challenging, rule-breaking characters who learnt through experience and were driven by their passions. Such people knew what they believed and acted upon it. When they encountered something that they felt was wrong, they did not just 'tut' or call the authorities; they confronted the transgressors with vehemence and sometimes violence. They even took on God when they felt he deserved it. They were frequently wrong, often misguided, but almost always sincere. They had an opinion that they could (and would) defend, because deep within them was a heart that they were not afraid to uncover, that they had not learnt to bind up.

Perhaps we should run through some examples. When Moses encounters God in the burning bush, he argues until, in the end, he makes God angry—but even then he gets his way and convinces God that appointing someone else as his actual mouthpiece would be a good idea.[5] Every time God asks Gideon to do something, he gets a question back. 'I am with you,' says God. 'If that's true, then how come you've left us in this mess?' retorts Gideon. 'Do what I say, and you will be successful,' God commands. 'Prove it!' Gideon repeatedly challenges him.[6] Abraham takes God to task over the injustice of his plan to destroy the immoral cities of Sodom and Gomorrah, rages against the idea of innocents being unfairly destroyed, and haggles over their lives, winning his argument.[7] Job also protests, accusing God of punishing the blameless and of mocking the innocent.[8]

We could go on, looking at the capricious David, the fiery Isaiah, and Elijah, who was not above a sarcastic mocking of his enemies. Jesus himself was capable of some pretty harsh and cutting words when he came across people of whom he did not approve, reserving his harshest criticism for the keepers of the Law.[9]

When it comes to being a child of God, the meek and mild stuff is not required. Our Father would prefer us to be genuine and challenging, prepared to be honestly and

---

[5]   Exodus 3—4
[6]   Judges 6—7
[7]   Genesis 18:17–33
[8]   Job 9
[9]   See, for example, Matthew 3:7; 21:44–46

outrageously wrong rather than quietly disapproving or, worse, lukewarm. In the letters to the seven churches in the book of Revelation, the toughest words are saved for the ambivalent congregation in the church at Laodicea: 'I know your deeds, that you are neither cold nor hot. I wish you were either one or the other! ... But you do not realise that you are wretched, pitiful, poor, blind and naked.'[10] He wants us to be bursting with personality and conviction. Those types of Bible characters sound attractive and charismatic, and I'd love my children to be like them. I know that sounds like a parenting nightmare—especially if we have to handle a lot of tantrums and disobedience—and there are days when I would prefer a quieter parenting life, but I believe that God wants us a little rougher round the edges.

I want to be clear that I am not calling us all to become more aggressive or suggesting that we should all be raising feisty children. In many cases, we will find that a quiet resolve is far more impressive than the heat of more extravert characters. I am simply suggesting that God rather expects us to run counter to the prevailing culture, and to do so confidently, without apologising for doing so. Far from expecting us to fit in, God asks us to be resilient in upholding our beliefs and our convictions. This can be done quietly—some might suggest, more effectively so—and one of the key parenting tasks is to support the confidence required when standing in the face of the resistance that it inevitably stirs up.

I want to tell my children that I am always there for them, and, with the exception of my human failings, I am—business trips notwithstanding. I don't mean that I travel around in their pockets. Sometimes I am with them, and sometimes

---

[10] Revelation 3:15–17

I need to let them do things on their own, but I want them to know that if ever they call or if ever they need me, I will be there. Sometimes, like during this business trip, my presence will have to be at the end of a phone, and I would prefer that not to be the case, but that is the limitation of our physical existence. The limitations of our humanity mean that sometimes they call and I am distracted or impatient or just too far away to be with them. The joy of having God as a Father is that he can be present when we call, but he knows the kind of child he is trying to develop. He knows that sometimes he will not answer our first call but will let us develop by having to endure alone, before eventually making it clear that he was there all the time.

Chapter Nine

Gentleness

The power and the glory

There is in God, some say,
A deep but dazzling darkness.

Henry Vaughan

All of my children love play-fighting with me, hurling their little bodies at me, bouncing off or being dragged down and tickled until they can hardly breathe. They get pinned to the floor, flung on to the sofa and lifted upside down, every time returning for more. The games would go on for ever if I didn't call a halt. I've noticed recently that they have also learnt to play-fight between themselves a little now. Most of these games end in tears, but only when one gets caught by a stray elbow or accidentally sits on another's arm. Generally speaking, it is all good fun, and I think it is quite an important part of their development. I don't mean that I think it is important for them to learn to fight, although I have nothing against the idea of kids training in any of the seemingly endless variety of martial arts now available. I hear that even boxing is making a comeback, and part of me thinks even that might be a good thing. I'm not especially keen on fighting as a sport, but an activity that allows children to explore their physical possibilities and to understand how their strength must be controlled within a framework of rules and respect makes sense to me.

Some of you may shrink from the idea of violence of any sort, but to deny that there is within creation a potentially crushing power is to ignore the bald facts. God, as well as being a God of beauty, poetry, artistry and peace, is also a God of limitless power. I well remember the day I was sitting in my office in Nepal, discussing budgets with Om Kar, my finance officer, when I heard a sound that made me stop and look up. It was a sound of malevolence and might, a roaring like an approaching jet engine but somehow more powerful, more threatening. My first thought was that a helicopter was landing on the roof, but it quickly became clear that, despite its volume, the sound was still some way off and approaching fast. Om Kar and I first looked at each other, both clearly bemused, and then we looked out of the window at a perfectly normal, humid and sultry day. Then, from the direction of the mountains, I saw it coming. It was like a vision of apocalypse—a turbulent grey wall rushing towards us across the fields. As it approached a small copse of trees, they started to thrash about in the wind that ran ahead of the cloud, beating against each other like tethered animals desperate to escape, and then they were engulfed and the roaring intensified.

The storm rushed on, and soon our building's roof and windows were clanging and banging as hail ricocheted against them. When the hail storm had passed, in perhaps five or ten minutes, the field outside was covered in tennis ball-sized lumps of ice, and the trees were still again, completely stripped of leaves. In the town where we lived, the largest hailstone that was found weighed over one and a half kilos, and cars everywhere had pock-marked roofs and bonnets as if they had been caught in crossfire. Windscreens were in short supply, the cracked glass all that remained once God had closed the doors of his meteorological storehouse.[1]

I'm happy to admit that, as I watched the approach of the storm, I was nervous. To see something of the power of God through his creation can inspire terror.[2] At other times, though, the show of naked power is beautiful. I've sat out in the Welsh hills with lightning slicing through the dark skies, even striking the ground nearby, and been thrilled by the experience. Many of us have watched the sea thrash against the shore and enjoyed the spectacle. If the whole world shouts about the personality of God, we can't admire the artistry in flowers and the majesty in mountains and then choose to ignore the vast forces in evidence, dwarfing anything that men and women at their technological zenith have achieved. Power and strength are part of God's personality.

When I fight my children, all of them under ten, there is no doubt in anyone's mind that if I wanted to hurt them, I could. In fact, I think they take great delight in feeling the strength within me that comes from being twice their size. There are times when they need that strength, to carry them when they are tired, to lift them on to walls and down from trees, to be a safe harbour to run to when they feel frightened. No matter what they call you to your face, in the playground they boast of your strength to their friends and enemies and draw confidence and status from their very association with you. They even promise that if a bully harms them, 'my dad will get you'. Not unlike Elijah,[3] children will trade comments about the relative strengths of their fathers, their access to resources, their power and influence.

---

[1]   Job 38:22–23

[2]   Job 37:4

[3]   1 Kings 18:27

I want to feel the same about my ˙God. If life can be characterised as a battle, sometimes physical, often emotional and always spiritual, then I want the big guns on my side. I want someone on my side who has legions to call on when it is time to fight, and I especially want someone who can protect me when I am outnumbered.[4] What, after all, is the point of taking refuge in a paper bag? If I am to acknowledge that spiritual forces beyond my reason are raging against me, and if in my hour of despair I am to call on my God, I want to know that the gentleness he often shows is not the limit of his power but evidence of his self-control. I may respect my God but I want my enemies to fear him with good cause.

Out of the strength came sweetness

Fear is that little darkroom where negatives are developed.
Michael Pritchard

Having said that, I want to admit something to you that is uncomfortable. I have had moments, just brief flashes, when I have wanted to lash out at my children and hurt them, and I believe that I am not alone in this. I've read books describing how new mothers, deprived of sleep and frustrated to the point of irrationality, have wanted to throw their crying baby at the wall. Once or twice, when grappling with my kids, one of them has gone too far and has hurt me. In that moment I know that my eyes flash with anger, and I see in the faces of my children that they, too, see a change come over me. To match my anger, I see fear register on their faces, and that is

---

[4]   Proverbs 18:10

enough to defuse the moment. Reconciliation follows: they are sorry that they have hurt me and I am sorry that I have frightened them.

These incidents are important to me because in them is, I believe, the true meaning of the gentleness of God—a gentleness that God wants to see developing within us as his children, and that I want to see developing in my own family. Gentleness is not the absolute absence of violence, or even the absence of the threat of it. Jesus was capable of being more than a little feisty in both words and actions.[5] A person who has no power is not gentle, but weak. Gentleness is not the absence of the potential for violence, but the degree to which power is controlled or withheld.

I am gentle with my children because I know that I can hurt them but I choose not to. Let me be clear that I do not regard physical harm as the only possible form of violence. For example, I hope that I don't parade my potential to injure them as a way to induce fear, for that too is violence. To decide to injure children, to nurture fear within them as a method of control, or to use adult experience or knowledge to manipulate or control them—all these things are forms of violence. They are wrong in any relationship, let alone the relationship between parent and child. Why, then, do I read so often that some Christians interpret natural disasters as punishment and judgment from God? This is a God who would have us cringe in fear before him like whimpering puppies before a cruel, whip-wielding master. That is not the God I recognise, yet versions of the caricature seem to persist.

It is easy to see any ill that befalls us as a sign of God's wrath—the punishment we deserve. If we are not careful, we

---

[5]   John 2:15–16

find ourselves succumbing to the temptation to ask, 'What have I done to deserve this?' Does that sound like effective parenting to you—to punish a child but leave them ignorant of the reason? It sounds closer to abuse to me, and I reject it as any sort of description of the behaviour of God as my Father. That he could direct his power against us is not in question, but that he chooses not to is the very expression of gentleness—strength under control; power applied appropriately and from the right motives.[6]

Spare the rod

Never raise your hand to your children—it leaves your mid-section unprotected.

Robert Orben

He that will have his son have a respect for him and his orders must himself have a great reverence for his son.

John Locke

We have already discussed the idea that if a father, whether God or a human parent, is too protective and quick to intervene to prevent any stress at all in his children's lives, it increases the likelihood of creating over-dependent children. We have also been clear that applying excessive punishment, whether verbal or physical, is the action of a brute. So what should our attitude be to discipline?

I'm not about to go toe-to-toe with James Dobson or any other child-rearing specialist, past or present; that is not the

---

[6] Psalm 86:15

point of this book. Again, though, my own experiences of parenting have helped me to think about the idea of God's discipline.

If my children do something wrong, there should be consequences, and those consequences should be both real and genuinely linked to the wrongdoing. Every parent will know that this principle is far harder to apply than it sounds. I well remember, in the days before we were married, my wife and I casually observing and commenting to one another about some misbehaving child at a restaurant table, battling with its parents, brilliantly pushing them to the limit of their patience while using their embarrassment as a weapon. My pet criticism at the time was about parents' over-use of the impotent threat. In some cases, it would be the repeated promise of a sanction that was never applied: for example, 'If you drop your fork on the floor again, I am going to take you straight home.' We've all seen it happen, and we all know that within two or three minutes the knife will be on the floor and, rather than ejecting the child, the parents will be embroiled in an argument about semantics.

'I told you not to do that.'

'You said if I dropped my *fork*.'

An alternative type of threat is the totally disproportionate one that is clearly never going to be carried out. 'I'm not going to let you spoil my meal,' the parent states, ignoring the fact that this has already happened. 'If you don't quieten down, I am going to lock you in the car outside.' No, they are not. I know it, they know it, and the child knows it. Finally, there is the threat so distantly removed from the current incident that it carries no weight at all: 'If you do that again, you will be banned from the PlayStation for a week.' In the child's mind, the two incidents are so unrelated that, if the threat is ever applied, it will create

95

more of a sense of injustice than a motivation to modify their behaviour in the restaurant.

Isolated from the scene by distance and lack of personal experience, I was able to observe smugly that all of these types of threat have one thing in common—their utter lack of efficacy. Now that I have my own children, I am able to report that I have repeatedly used all of these tactics myself, and I was right: they don't work. I'm not convinced, either, that the use of a wooden spoon to smack my children when I get them home will be any more effective, although I've never tried that one. (Sorry, James Dobson.)

Actually, what seems to work best (although by no means universally) in modifying poor behaviour is an understanding of its consequences, although some explanation is often required when the effect is significantly distant from the cause. When the babysitter is booked and the children ask why they can't come with you to the restaurant, that could be the time to explain to them that their behaviour at the last meal spoilt the experience and so this time you have decided not to take them. Quite often, however, no explanation is necessary. Children who play with their toys recklessly break them and, as long as the toys are not instantly replaced, they have to cope with the loss. If they don't play fairly with friends or siblings, they soon find themselves playing on their own. (In fact, in these situations I sometimes think that the intervention of parents to try to 'make' the kids play nicely together rather prolongs the difficulty; more often than not, the children seem to sort out these problems themselves.) The occasions when children seem most ready to receive input from parents are the times when they come with questions. 'Why don't they want to play with me?' or 'Why can't we come to dinner with you?' provide excellent opportunities for a little parental input on issues of behaviour.

Of course, I'm over-simplifying and there are indeed some situations in which parents rightly do not want their children to experience consequences as a learning aid. I'm sure that, having severed a finger, a youngster will learn new respect . for sharp knives, but the price seems a little heavy, to say the least—so we have to intervene to protect them.

The question is, then, whether all this can help us as we reflect on God's responses to our own errant behaviour. You see, much as some people like to caricature God as a fearsome, lightning-wielding disciplinarian, prepared to answer each indiscretion with a sudden flash, the Bible suggests that sin carries its own punishment within, pre-packaged: very clearly, sin brings death.[7] At the same time, God has made it clear that he has provided a route for us to escape the consequences of sin, no matter how often we transgress. There is no system of 'penalty points on the licence' where sin is concerned: if there were, a one-off minor offence might go relatively unnoticed, and only repeated or major misdemeanours would have eternal consequences. Instead, the sentence from which we are reprieved is identical, no matter what the perceived scale of the crime.

The ultimate punishment for sin is one that the Father feels at least as keenly as do his children, and probably infinitely more so, for that punishment is separation from him. Often, we focus on the idea that separation from God is our loss—as indeed it is—but rarely do we consider the loss that God would feel, as a parent, if he had to be separated from one of his children. It may be easier for us to understand that he would go to almost any lengths to rescue us if we consider what we, as parents, might be prepared to do if we were

---

[7]   Romans 6:23

faced with the prospect of living without our children.

God, to his and our joy, had a solution. The punishment has already been meted out: God the Father and God the Son endured the agony of separation from each other.[8] The price having been paid, God has now moved on. I therefore do not subscribe to the concept that we may be punished further by God for our misdemeanours. Yet it is hard for many people to avoid the semi-superstitious thought that any misfortune they are enduring is because of some unconnected wrong that they have committed. Like a football supporter wondering if the team lost this week because he forgot to phone home on his mother's birthday, Christians can feel as if their poor 'luck' is deserved. To hold to this belief, though, suggests that Jesus' sacrifice was not enough—that it was an imperfect settlement, only an initial payment, and that there is somehow more to be paid.

It is certainly true that our mistakes or misdemeanours have their own consequences, which we have to live with— just as a child who wilfully breaks a toy in a fit of pique has to do without it. When we damage a relationship through lies or deceit, we have to deal with the broken relationship: we have to either work to repair it or live with the scars. We may ask God to repair or replace the relationship and interpret his failure to do so as a punishment. But if a parent instantly replaced any broken toy, by whatever means it was destroyed, would we not interpret that action as spoiling the child? Rather, if the child recognises what she has done and asks for the parent's help in repairing the breakage, a good parent will settle down alongside the child, encourage her to glue some of the pieces together and provide help

---

8   Mark 15:34

when the job is clearly beyond her competence.

In the same way, perhaps we should interpret the actions of God in response to our errors as a way of supporting us in repairing what we can. God does not need to punish us, even for the errors that he has warned us against, because, as we have said, the sacrifice of Jesus is sufficient. He prefers to support and discipline us through the learning and development that result from living with and rectifying our mistakes as best we can.[9]

A repaired toy is not the same as a new one, and it may bear cracks as reminders of our foolishness, but the smears of glue also remind us of the times we worked side by side with our father. In many cases, it may become more precious and better loved precisely because it is not pristine: the joins are a testimony to the effort required to patch and repair. Just as the toy is not discarded, so we are not abandoned by our heavenly Father. The relationship is restored; we are healed. Something that endures a painful break, and is fixed through an investment of time and love, can become more highly treasured than something unblemished.

---

[9]   Proverbs 3:12

·:·

Chapter Ten

Self-control

'P's and 'Q's

Children need models rather than critics.

Joseph Joubert

'What do you say?'

'Thank you.'

How many times have you heard or participated in that little scenario? How many times a day have you demanded the 'magic word' or held back from handing something over until your children have asked for it 'properly'? It's as if, with toddlers, there is a kind of Pavlovian stimulus–response training going on as we try to teach them some of the basic points of etiquette. Our assumption seems to be that if we force them to repeat 'thank you' often enough, it will eventually become automatic, delivered without thought or meaning. Surely nowhere, with perhaps the exception of Canada, can this be more the case than in England, where we thank people for treading on our toes or apologise when they obstruct us. As a consequence, we are delighted when, in company, our children say the right thing and we are complimented for having such polite progeny. Of course, they may not really be grateful, and when they say 'thank you' for that hideous gift from an aunt they only meet once every other year, we are actually encouraging false gratitude, but it saves us from embarrassment.

The problem with etiquette is that, although it is founded on simple principles of respect and consideration for the people we encounter in our daily lives, these are difficult concepts to communicate adequately to our young children. Furthermore, the social norms that develop from these basic principles are so complicated, and predicated on such a detailed understanding of the appropriate responses to any given situation, that it is far easier to play safe and provide a simple set of rules for children to obey. For example, I don't say 'thank you' to my wife absolutely every time she hands me an item. Sometimes I do say it sarcastically, when she hands me something I don't want, but the fear that my children might copy me and give an ironic 'Yeah, thanks!' to the aforementioned aunt is enough to wake me up in a cold sweat on the eve of our biennial visit.

I remember one occasion when we had a friend coming to stay, whom we had not seen for at least a couple of years. When my daughter was small, this friend had lived very near us and had often come to babysit, and my daughter had become especially fond of her. Now, however, Zoë was struggling to remember who the friend was, and my wife was trying to describe her. Zoë's memory was not jogged by her hair colour or her name, so Morna tried one other characteristic that might stick in a small child's mind: 'She's quite fat.' That didn't do the trick, as it turned out, but, reassuringly, when our friend arrived Zoë instantly recognised her. All was going well until lunch on the second day, just before our friend was due to leave, when Zoë offered this comment across the table: 'Mummy, she's not actually very fat.'

The friend has never visited again. It is just so hard to teach your children the concept of appropriate speech. So, although I might choose when to say 'thank you', I prefer my children to have a simple rule to follow; although I might leave the table when I judge it to be appropriate, I like my children to ask before they get down. The rules are there to make life easier until they develop a sense of the right way to behave in the vast majority of situations, and the skills to make their own assessment when they are faced with a new circumstance. While the rules give them a framework within which they can operate safely, let's not pretend that training them to say 'thank you' does anything to help them develop a genuine sense of gratitude.

God has provided us with some fairly simple rules for good living: we have already mentioned some of the prohibitions, such as adultery, murder, lying and so on. Similarly, the rules we set for our children are designed not to be a burden but to act as basic guidance. However, Jesus wanted to take us a stage further, so he explained that God does not want blind obedience to the rules, any more than we do when our children grow up. He was keen for us to understand that living well is not about following the rules but more about grasping the principles behind them. The two 'greatest commandments' are, in fact, the principles, and the other commands are simple prohibitions based on them. If we love and respect God, and love and respect other people, the rest will follow.[1]

Do as I do, not (just) as I say

Never take the advice of someone who has not had your kind of trouble.

Sydney J. Harris

---

[1]   Matthew 22:36–40

Ultimately, whatever rules we set out for our children, we ourselves may break them. We tell them never to lie and then explain that their Christmas presents come from Santa Claus; we tell them never to snatch and then grab the sharp knife from them before they can hurt themselves. We don't want to break our own rules but, because they never seem to cover every eventuality—because we don't set perfect rules—we sometimes feel the need to escape them. In some ways, this is a good thing if we want our children to move on from simply following the rules and start to apply the principles, to become their own people. We'd rather see them exhibit genuine gratitude than parrot their thanks; we'd rather see them develop meaningful and close relationships than adhere to strict etiquette at all times. They will not learn these things from our rules; they will learn them from our example. As they grow to understand not just what we do but why we do it, they too will develop a moral compass, which will help to guide them more successfully than any list of prescribed or proscribed actions. Jesus himself made it clear that applying the rule book is no way to guide people, even if it ensures that we have their respect.[2] Unfortunately, teaching by example is no easy thing: if we exhibit unhealthy behaviour or warped morality, that will be passed on, no matter what we say.

Our adolescent children will decide how to behave by following their inner voice, their conscience, which has developed over a period of time through watching the lives of those they love and respect. They make mistakes but, more often than not, the faults that we perceive are distorted reflections of our own examples. Our children become a chip off the old block, and we may smile in recognition as we see this happening.

---

[2]   Matthew 23:4

I believe that God also smiles when he sees us take some responsibility, and applauds when he sees a reflection of his own qualities in our actions. We've been designed with a conscience, and the degree to which we exercise self-control is not a measure of the existence of that inner voice or, indeed, our ability to hear it. Rather, our self-control shows in our deliberate decision to follow it. If we have allowed God to participate in the development of our conscience, by making time and space to reflect on his personality and characteristics, the fruit of this process is the development of God's characteristics within us. The final part of the fruit of the Spirit is self-control—becoming mature enough that we can intentionally decide to follow what we know to be right. If we are self-controlled, we find ourselves ready to stand against the voices suggesting that it would be easier or more profitable to follow what we know to be wrong choices. We come to recognise those voices for what they are—the whisperings of evil temptation.

We were created and born to be free, to take responsibility, to exert control over ourselves. God is proud of his children when they do this. The alternative is to become selfish—submissive to and controlled by the self.[3]

Praise

If the only prayer you said in your whole life was 'thank you', that would suffice.

Meister Eckhart

---

[3] Ephesians 2:3

Parents talk of the need to spend 'quality time' with their children: sometimes they excuse the snatched moments spent with their children by reassuring themselves that when they are together, it is still quality time. Of course, I've suggested already that the only way to get quality time is to have quantity time. In my experience, this is true, but I have also noticed that it does not have to involve the parent abandoning their own agenda to focus on what the children want to do. In fact, I think that some of the best quality and quantity time comes when children abandon their play and spend some time getting involved with the parent's agenda.

I've often noticed, for example, that all my children love to spend time with me, doing whatever I am doing, even though it may be something of a chore to me. Most Saturday afternoons I find myself with my two youngest children, and for a time they are happy if I play with them, bouncing on the trampoline or fiddling around with small action figures. More than that, though, they enjoy helping me do some job or other, especially if I arrange the task so that they can take part. As a consequence, washing the car takes far longer than it would if I did it on my own because I have to find extra sponges and a box for them to stand on, and allow them to control the hose. When it comes to DIY, they can bring progress to a standstill as I let them make a saw cut, hammer in a nail or measure up. Jed loves to hold the steel tape, while Zoë loves to write down measurements. A simple job can feel as if it will take for ever—a case of quality and quantity time!

Just last month, we decided to creosote the shed. The tin warned about the consequences of splashes on the skin and made it quite clear that I should not allow the mixture anywhere near my children, but that wouldn't do because they wanted to help. So for the first 20 minutes we hunted for waterproof coats and made sure that overtrousers were tucked into wellington boots. Hoods were pulled up and plastic bags were turned into makeshift gloves, held in place with string. When we finally got going, the children looked more like nuclear physicists than painters. It meant, though, that we could set about painting the shed, drawing circles and painting them over, getting splashed with the brown fluid and becoming generally mucky. They lost interest three-quarters of the way through, necessitating a pause for undressing and washing before I could finish off the job, but when it was finally done they could stand with me and admire our handiwork.

Thinking back on the experience, I reckon it was a pretty good approximation to worship. The requirement that God's people should praise him is one aspect of faith that, if we are honest, we find a bit peculiar. Why on earth are we commanded to love him, as if love can be commanded in any case? While erotic love may flare up in an instant (and die down just as quickly), other expressions of love tend to develop over time spent together: you can't force them. Simply going through the motions seems at best disingenuous—unless it is done to help rekindle a love that has somehow faded. Then there does seem to be a 'chicken-and-egg' relationship between our emotions and actions, which means that living as if you are in love can help the feeling to return.

Why, then, does God command us to worship him? If he is insecure, needing constant reminders that we think he is actually quite good, I'm not sure he fits my understanding of a complete and perfect God. The idea that his ego may require a massage is as unhealthy as the idea of a parent depending on their children for a sense of self-worth.

I would rather think about worship as deliberately spending time with God, watching what he is doing and, where he allows, getting involved with it. That, for me, has a point, unlike simply saying, 'God, you are wonderful.' The point may well be to understand another facet of his personality and, in doing so, appreciate him better. My children appreciate my DIY skills (such as they are) when they get involved. Sometimes they even compliment me on them. In the same way, deliberately getting involved with the work of God stirs something in my heart and, without a conscious effort, I find that I am offering him genuine heartfelt praise. For my children, one of the byproducts of spending time with me, doing my work, is that it helps them develop a healthy respect for me, based on a better understanding of who I am and what I can do. From this respect comes a desire to emulate me, and this in turn helps to provide a motivation to develop their own abilities. If worship is the process of developing a better understanding of who God is and what he can do, then the natural extension of this will be a deepening respect both for him and for his authority, an appreciation of the wisdom that lies behind his advice and his instruction.

For me, worship is far more than singing songs; it can be preparing and delivering a sermon that requires me to look hard at a Bible passage and think through what it really means. It can be supporting a friend through real difficulties by talking through the issues or just spending time together. For others, it could be working with young people, either in a church context or in the community, or aiming to get an element of their company profits diverted towards the support of suitable charities. Whatever the activity, a practical task needs prayer, requires us to think about what God might be doing in each circumstance, and forces us to reflect on our understanding of the way God works. I always finish such a task appreciating him better.

God clearly doesn't need my help: if he did all the work himself without any human intervention, he would undoubtedly make faster progress. The point of this collaboration, though, is that it develops within us the love, joy, peace, patience, kindness, goodness, faithfulness and gentleness that are the characteristics of God. We see the Father's likeness forming in us, his children. With those values firmly in place within us, he asks us to exercise them all, to take control of ourselves. One day my children will be adults. They will not have to obey the rules of my house but will be free to set their own agendas. When they do, I hope I will be able to send them out with my blessing, proud of them and confident that they leave well-equipped. That's what fathers do.

❖

Conclusion

Lost and found

Can there be an experience more painful or desperate than outliving a son or daughter? I have a number of friends who have lived to see their children die, some as babies, others as adults in their own right. I've never experienced it myself and I hope against hope that I never do. Can there be a loss more profound? Can there be a single parent who has never feared such a circumstance? Many people of little or no faith have found themselves praying for the safe return of a child who has slipped away on the beach or been lost from sight amid a crowd of shoppers. All parents of older children have sat up in bed, waiting to hear the reassuring guilty creep of late-night feet on the stairs, or have chewed nails away during the first journey at the wheel of a car after the 'L' plates have been discarded. Happily, most of these anxious moments are just temporary, but newspapers testify to the fact that sometimes children don't return, and the knowledge that this has happened to a very few heightens the fears of all of us.

I sometimes think that worry is one of the very few human emotions that God must only be able to guess at. If God exists outside time, how can he possibly worry? It must be like watching a film for the second time—still enjoying the experience, empathising with the characters, even crying with them in their dark moments, but never worrying about how it will all turn out. No, I don't think it can be possible for God to worry as we do.

Before you envy God his lack of agitated, jaw-clenching fear, consider this: if God has no worry, surely it is replaced with the absolute certainty that he will lose a great many of his children. In some of his relationships, God's experience can perhaps be more closely likened to that of the parent with a terminally ill child, trying hard to enjoy time with the child while they are together, and being doubly hurt by the child's rejections and tantrums, because there is the certain heavy knowledge that these precious moments are all that they will have together. Soon, too soon, they will be gone. For some of his children, God knows with certainty that the outcome will be separation and loss. Do you think the fact that so many children do return to the Father and choose to live with him lessens his sense of loss over those who go away, never to return? I don't know the answer. I haven't the courage to ask a parent who has lost an only child to compare their experience to that of the parent who has lost one of several. I suspect that whatever small comfort one may draw from the surviving children is dwarfed by the sense of loss.

Among all their other emotions, the parents of missing or dying children experience powerfully the sense of impotence. If there was something, anything they could do, no matter what the cost, they would do it. They would donate their own organs, even sacrifice their own lives, perhaps because they sense that life without their child will be almost un-bearable—no more than existence, all colour replaced by grey. Last year, a cousin of mine was killed in a car accident. The funeral was on a bright blue December day, and it was a wonderful celebration of her life, loves and passions, held in a church full of a peculiar mixture of sadness and celebration as many, many relatives and friends remembered her. She, of course, is completely at rest and feels no pain or sadness whatsoever. That peace is, I am sad to say, in stark contrast to the feelings of her parents and sister, who I know have genuinely questioned if they will ever laugh again without it sounding hollow. I believe that if any one of them could give up their life to bring her back, they would do it, not least because in many senses they have had to give up the life they had anyway. Life without her feels so much less than it was supposed to feel.

Only perhaps in those terms can we understand the idea of God choosing to sacrifice his Son. From his out-of-time perspective, God knew at the moment of creation the loss that would also come if he did not find a way to bring back at least some of his children. Bringing us into being solely for the purpose of relationship, he was prepared to do anything necessary to avoid an eternal knowledge of what could have been.

In order to save his children, God took the extraordinary decision to become one of his children. While an earthly parent may understand that a father would give up his own life for his son, we can't begin to grasp the idea that, in doing so, God also gave up one Son's life for his many other children[1] I have tried to clarify some of my understanding of God by looking at my experience of fatherhood, but this reminds me that human experience can only provide, at best, hints and glimpses of a God who cannot be fully explained.

In a similar way, even the joys of human parenthood cannot fully reflect the joy that we will experience when we are finally reunited with God. Even Jesus, that master of metaphor, comes short of a perfect description of that moment: it is hard to believe that a shepherd's joy over finding one of his sheep quite matches the rejoicing in heaven when a sinner

---

[1] John 3:16

repents![2] Perhaps the closest we may come is to imagine the hope that bereaved parents have of meeting their children again in heaven.

Much of this book has focused on the earthly parent's role in nurturing the child to mature into a strong, confident adult, ready to take a full and active role in society. During the years of transition from baby through toddler and teenager to young adult, the relationship between parent and child necessarily changes to meet the young person's needs. At no point in this journey or, indeed, beyond it into the child's adulthood does the father relinquish his role. Now that I am an adult, I understand my own father better than I ever did before; if anything (even though I am now, in many areas of life, more capable than he), I have more respect for him than ever.

I see my time on earth in similar terms, as a two-stage journey. The first stage is like the developmental path through childhood—learning and growing, attempting to absorb the lessons of life and assume more of the characteristics of a fully mature Christian who will be ready eventually to take his place in the full presence of God. The second part of the journey, inseparable from the first, is a deepening understanding of who God is. This too will be truly complete only in heaven, but I increasingly find that the more I understand, the more I recognise my ignorance and the more I desire to know. I accept fully that this will mean I may have to rewrite this whole book in ten years' time! I may one day challenge some of the conclusions I have drawn here, but that will make this step in my journey no less valuable.

I offer these reflections to you in the hope that they will

---

[2] Luke 15:7

encourage you in your journey to full Christian maturity, and that they will help you challenge your assumptions about the nature of your heavenly Father. You may agree with me or you may disagree, but if I have caused you to feel just once that there might be a side to God that you had not previously considered, we will both have learnt something. More than that, I hope I have encouraged you to look at your children, your father and your other relationships and simply to wonder what else within them might provide fresh clues to the character of God. I believe with all my heart that if you look with an open mind and a receptive heart, you will find his fingerprints everywhere.

✤

Some thoughts on using this book

For individuals

Because this book is written primarily for men, I have assumed that it is more likely to be read by individuals than as a study guide for groups. I've tried to break the book down into chapters and subchapters that will allow you, if you wish, to read a short section at a time. Including the introduction and the conclusion, there are 29 subsections, each headed by a brief title and in most cases by a quotation. If taken one at a time, these should provide you with enough bite-sized reflections to support a month of morning devotions.

I'd like to encourage you to use the subsections as a springboard to help you consider your own experiences and how they might shape and challenge your assumptions about God. You may find that having a Bible with you, and following a routine similar to the one below, helps you to put aside 30 minutes in your day to focus on God.

1. Take five minutes to ask God to reveal something new about himself to you today.
2. Read the subsection heading and the quotation. Pause to think a little about the quotation. Most of them are by authors who would not necessarily regard themselves as Christians, but this book encourages you to seek God even in less conventional places.

3. Read the subsection. They do vary in length, but none should take more than ten minutes to read.
4. If any part strikes you particularly, take the time to look up the Bible references in the footnotes. Feel free to challenge my conclusions with your own, but also aim to identify where your perception of God is based on assumptions and where it is based on sound evidence from the scriptures. Consider how your personal experience of fatherhood (as a child or a father) complements or contradicts this evidence.
5. Pray, asking God to show you more about this aspect of his personality in the coming day.

For groups

It will surprise and delight me if small groups use this book as part of their programme. I want to make it clear that the book is not designed to provide 'right' answers, but would be better used as a catalyst to stimulate debate. For this reason, I would strongly suggest that those leading the group take time in the introductory meeting to emphasise that the objective is to help people confront the assumptions they may hold about God. Ask people to be open to one another's views and opinions, and make sure that all members of the group feel safe in exploring personal experiences. Remember that, for some people, being asked to reflect on their own experiences as a parent or child can be extremely challenging.

The book is divided into ten chapters and broadly uses the fruit of the Spirit (Galatians 5:22–23) as a guiding text. The following plan may be helpful for a ten-week course based on the main chapters. It would be helpful if, each week, the group members could have read the identified chapters ahead of the meeting.

It may also be helpful to have a reasonably standard format to each session, based on the following outline:

- **Share:** This is an opportunity for all to share what they found challenging or interesting about the chapter, where they agreed or disagreed with the author and how their own experiences support or counter the conclusions.
- **Read:** A key relevant Bible passage is highlighted for review in the group.
- **Reflection:** This is a question to consider from the passage.
- **Prayer:** An opportunity is offered to pray for a revelation of the specific character of God being discussed, or to pray for group members who may need support in dealing with the issues raised by the chapter.

Week One: Introduction and Knowing God

- **Read:** Introduction and Chapter One
- **Share:** Discuss how members of the group feel about the concept of unconditional love. Do they feel capable of accepting it?
- **Read:** Genesis 22:1–19
- **Reflection:** Having read the passage, consider how well Abraham knew God or must have known God. Consider how this experience may have changed Abraham's relationship with God.
- **Prayer:** Pray in the group, asking God to help each member develop a deeper understanding of the personality of God.

Week Two: Love

- **Read**: Chapter Two
- **Share**: How well do the group members feel they know God? What aspects of God do they find puzzling? What aspects do they find difficult to understand, which are just assumed to be true by the Church? How does the use of the word 'father' help or hinder their understanding of God?
- **Read**: Matthew 5:43–48
- **Reflection**: Is it possible to love unconditionally? Is it possible to accept unconditional love?
- **Prayer**: Pray for an ability to accept the unconditional love of God. Encourage members to pray (silently or aloud) for people they struggle to love.

Week Three: Joy

- **Read**: Chapter Three
- **Share**: What activity helps the group members best to experience real joy? How do they feel about these activities?
- **Read**: Psalm 149
- **Reflection**: Consider what it is about you that might delight God. How does that make you feel?
- **Prayer**: Pray in the group, asking God to release each member to express themselves and develop joyful lives.

Week Four: Peace

- **Read**: Chapter Four
- **Share**: When do members of the group feel most at peace? What robs them of peace?
- **Read**: Matthew 6:25–34
- **Reflection**: How easy is it to follow the instruction not to worry? How easy is it to trust the promise of God, that he will provide?
- **Prayer**: Pray in the group or individually about the areas of life that rob members of peace, and ask for faith and trust in God's promise to provide.

Week Five: Patience

- **Read**: Chapter Five
- **Share**: Ask the group to share times where they have experienced unanswered prayer. Does this lead them to question God's priorities or God's promises? What causes them to become impatient with God?
- **Read**: Jeremiah 29:4–14
- **Reflection**: How did the exiles receive Jeremiah's prophecy, do you imagine?
- **Prayer**: Pray in the group, asking God to help individuals look for areas where they may better discern God's priorities.

Week Six: Kindness

- **Read**: Chapter Six
- **Share**: Where do members of the group find themselves competing with others? Is it healthy or unhealthy competition? What does 'abundance mentality' mean in practical terms to the group?
- **Read**: 2 Corinthians 9:6–15
- **Reflection**: How can we develop a spirit of cheerful giving?
- **Prayer**: Ask God to point out areas where members struggle to give or where they feel the need to compete selfishly.

Week Seven: Goodness

- **Read**: Chapter Seven
- **Share**: In the group members' minds, how does God view them? Do they feel as if he sees them as good? How easy do members find it to confess their wrongdoing?
- **Read**: Proverbs 28:13–14
- **Reflection**: This may be a good session in which to celebrate Communion together. Focus especially on the act of preparing for Communion and the confession of sins.
- **Prayer**: After Communion, pray together (either silently or aloud), thanking God for the gift of confession and forgiveness.

Week Eight: Faithfulness

- Read: Chapter Eight
- Share: Having read the chapter, where do group members feel challenged about their own ability to be faithful in a countercultural manner? Where do they feel it is easier to fit in than to stand out? How well does the Church in general stand out faithfully?
- Read: Psalm 139
- Reflection: How do members of the group feel about being totally known by God?
- Prayer: Ask for strength in dealing with issues where the Christian culture runs against the prevailing culture for group members at home, work, school or in other areas.

Week Nine: Gentleness

- Read: Chapter Nine
- Share: How do group members feel about the idea of a powerful God? How do they feel they might be disciplined as disciples of Christ?
- Read: Job 38
- Reflection: What comfort can be drawn from this picture of God?
- Prayer: The end of the chapter looks at the idea that people or relationships may be broken as a consequence of sin. Remembering that these relationships can be repaired and may become more precious as a result, provide an opportunity for group members to seek healing.

Week Ten: Self-control and Conclusion

- **Read**: Chapter Ten and Conclusion
- **Share**: What helps the group members to worship? Conversely, what do they find difficult about worship? What activities help them to focus on God and recognise him for who he is?
- **Read**: John 3:16
- **Reflection**: Use the verse to help the group think again about the nature of their relationship with God as a child with a parent. Think especially about what they would do for their children (if they have any) and, correspondingly, how God must feel about them.
- **Prayer**: Use this time to worship God. In particular, thank him for aspects of his personality that may have struck you through looking at him from the perspective of fatherhood/parenthood.

Also by Brad Lincoln

Six Men Encountering God

This is a book of stories—shared by six quite different men. Meet the rock climber facing a fatal fall, the wheeler-dealer whose life goes belly-up, the cynic whose prejudices are confounded, and the others who share with them a pivotal experience. Each one, in a moment of crisis or by a process of gradual realisation, recognises a God-shaped gap within. Discovering this gap and then meeting the God who fills it ends up making all the difference in the world...

Read these stories, get acquainted with the men themselves, and draw your own conclusions about the nature of the God who reveals himself in Jesus. You may feel you know this God well or you may doubt that he exists at all, but if these stories do anything, they will certainly act as a reminder that God knows us. He knows you. In fact, he is getting involved with you, intervening in your life even now. After all, what made you pick up this book in the first place?

ISBN 978 1 84101 528 6   £6.99
Available from your local Christian bookshop or, in case of difficulty, direct from BRF using the order form on page 127.

Good Enough Mother

God at work in the challenge of parenting

Naomi Starkey

From the first delightful, daunting shock when we welcome a child into our lives, things are never the same again. And as the years speed by, the parenting adventure does not come to an end but simply changes. Even if our 'children' are now older than we were when they were born, and taller and wiser than we ever imagined, we never stop being their mothers. But do we ever feel good enough or really up to the job?

This is not a 'how to parent' book, but one that explores the emotional and spiritual side of mothering. Looking at a number of challenges common to many mothers' experience, it considers how God can be at work even in the most discouraging situations, to grow his fruit in our hearts and bring us the peace and joy that we often feel we lack. Knowing that our heavenly Father is guiding us in the awesome task that he has entrusted to us, we can find that, after all, we do have the confidence to be the mothers he has called us to be.

ISBN 978 1 84101 612 2   £5.99
Available from your local Christian bookshop or, in case of difficulty, direct from BRF using the order form on page 127.

Also from BRF

Running the Race Marked Out for Us

Lessons from Hebrews 12

Andrew Wooding Jones

Although events such as the London Marathon grow in popularity year after year, with athletes training to beat their personal best and raise money for charity, the general assumption today is that when things get tough, it is much easier to give up than press on through the pain barrier. Persevering is not a popular idea—but that is exactly what God calls his followers to do, as this book spells out.

In a verse-by-verse exploration of one of the New Testament's most inspiring passages, this book invites us on the challenge of a lifetime—the race of faith, which we run in the company of a 'cloud of witnesses' who urge us on as we follow in the footsteps of Jesus. Based on a discipleship course at Ashburnham Place, it reveals a wealth of encouragement and hope in Hebrews 12, and reminds us of all that we are called to do and be, as sons and daughters of God.

ISBN 978 1 84101 527 9   £5.99
Available from your local Christian bookshop or, in case of difficulty, direct from BRF using the order form on page 127.

Also from BRF

Growing Leaders

Reflections on leadership, life and Jesus

James Lawrence

Seven out of ten Christian leaders feel overworked, four in ten suffer financial pressures, only two in ten have had management training, and 1500 give up their job over a ten-year period. At the same time, as financial restrictions affect the availability of full-time ministers, more people are needed for leadership roles in local congregations, for every area of church work.

This book faces the challenge of raising up new leaders and helping existing leaders to mature, using the model for growing leaders at the heart of the Arrow Leadership Programme, a ministry of the Church Pastoral Aid Society (CPAS). It comprehensively surveys leadership skills and styles, discerning our personal calling, avoiding the 'red zone' of stress, developing character, and living as part of the community of God's people.

ISBN 978 1 84101 246 9   £8.99
Available from your local Christian bookshop or, in case of difficulty, direct from BRF using the order form on page 127.